EILEEN'S

THE LEGACY OF THE FILTER ROOM

EILEEN YOUNGHUSBAND

Published by
Candy Jar Books
Mackintosh House
136 Newport Road, Cardiff, CF24 1DJ
www.candyjarbooks.co.uk

ISBN: 978-0-9935192-2-2

Edited by Lauren Thomas & Shaun Russell
Editorial: Hayley Cox & Andy Frankham-Allen
Cover by Will Brooks & Jason Goy
Special thanks to Hugh Turnbull & Richard Young

I dedicate this children's book to my great grandson Colin Clive Booth in the hope that his generation will not forget the difficulties and dangers we faced and overcame when threatened by Hitler and his forces in 1939.

INTRODUCTION

My book, *One Woman's War,* was written to tell the story of the Airwomen of the RAF who worked during World War Two in the secret Filter Room. They were covered by the Official Secrets Act and could not tell anyone any details of their vital contribution to the air defence of our country until thirty years after peace was declared.

It is time to write it in terms which can better be understood by young people.

With this in mind, I have rewritten it in the hope it will be a record of the contribution these young women made in the defeat of Hitler and his armies and the preservation of our nation. I hope this will never be forgotten.

CHAPTER ONE

Imagine having to make a bar of chocolate last seven days. Do you think you could do it? Would you be able to resist peeling back the wrapper and gobbling up the whole thing?

Lots of foods were rationed during World War Two eggs, milk, sugar, and meat.

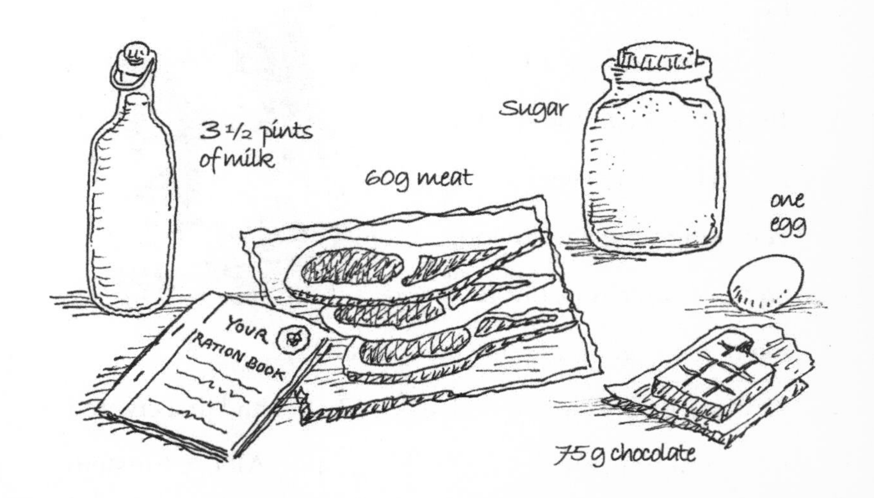

I usually looked forward to the rations of chocolate the most. I remember rushing to the local shop on a Monday morning to collect the food rations for the week, and then desperately trying to make it last.

Perhaps you're expecting my story to be boring, just an old lady yabbering on about how different the olden days were. Things *were* very different back then, but different doesn't mean boring. I've had a fair few adventures in my time.

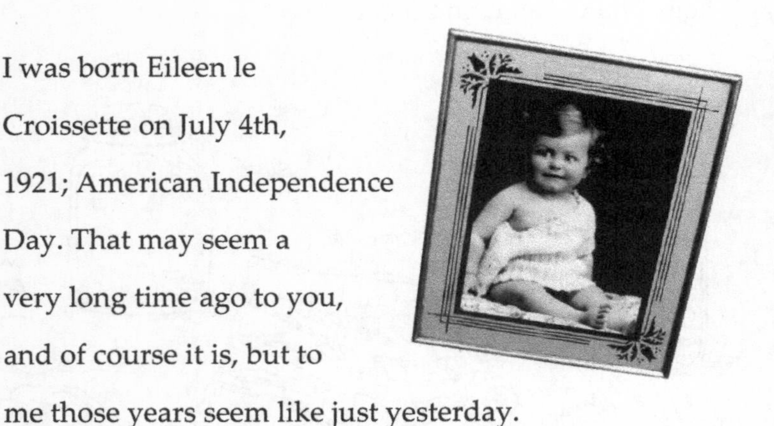

I was born Eileen le Croissette on July 4th, 1921; American Independence Day. That may seem a very long time ago to you, and of course it is, but to me those years seem like just yesterday.

King George V reigned, Coco Chanel had just created her iconic perfume Chanel No.5, and Albert Einstein would be awarded the Nobel Prize that year. If you are good at maths, you will have worked out that I have been around for more than ninety years – someday I might even receive a letter from the Queen on my 100th birthday.

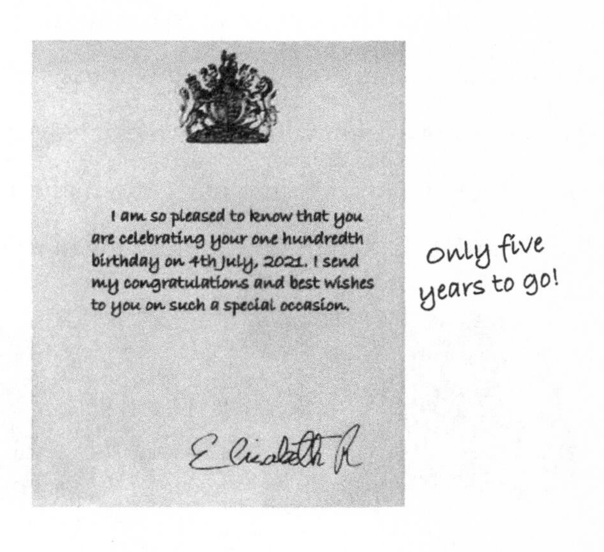

I am so pleased to know that you are celebrating your one hundredth birthday on 4th July, 2021. I send my congratulations and best wishes to you on such a special occasion.

Elizabeth R

But let's not get ahead of ourselves.

I grew up in an ordinary semi-detached house in Winchmore Hill in London with my mother and father, my younger brother Dennis and my mother's parents. We were lucky to have parents who encouraged us both to learn as much as we could, take chances and to make the most of our lives. My mother was in charge of the money, and worked at the counting house at a boutique on Bond Street. My father was a craftsman. He worked as a cabinet maker and joiner, and he did everything for my brother and me. He made us toys, cut our hair, swept the chimney and mended things in the house.

I remember one night when I was ten or eleven, when my father took me outside into our garden and pointed out the different stars in the sky, telling me their names.

My parents used to take us to lots of places, we went

to local parks and museums, but my favourite place to visit was the library, filled with rows and rows of towering bookshelves. I wanted to read them all. My brother and I were always curious children, eager to learn about the world around us. The library served as a wonderful gateway to stories of explorers and inventors and kings of old. I learned to treasure books, and the words these people had written. Perhaps it was these visits that influenced Dennis and I to go on and write books ourselves.

We both had music lessons when we were still in school, but my brother was the real musician. I could play a few tunes on the piano but, although I could read music, I found it hard work and never really mastered it. Dennis, however, played the violin beautifully and got great pleasure out of it. I remember that he would practice for hours, entertaining my parents with the latest piece he'd learned. Although Dennis and I were good friends when we were young, we were very different in some ways. Perhaps that was the first sign that we would take very different paths in our lives.

I always took an interest in maths and languages, like French and German, but Dennis was very good at science.

In fact, he went on to be an engineer for NASA in the United States, designing tools that were very important to astronauts when they went on missions to space. It always sounded so exciting. Dennis became the manager of NASA's Surveyor program ahead of the famous Apollo Moon landing mission.

He designed special instruments which were fitted on the Surveyor probe; a kind of robot that tested the soil on the Moon's surface and its atmosphere to ensure it was safe for landing. Dennis also designed another space vehicle for the Mariner program which tried to land on Mars.

Surveyor Probe

I remember receiving a phone call from him in America, telling me that an astronaut had found some of his instruments on a nearby Surveyor, and was bringing them back to California to be tested and analysed. I will always be so proud of my younger brother – that little boy who used to run around the library with me as a child looking for stories about kings and explorers, who went on to create such incredible things. It comforts me that there are still machines that he designed sitting on the Moon today; his part in history.

CHAPTER TWO

When I was in school, everybody learning German had a pen-friend from a similar school in Germany, so I had started writing to Werner Eisner. He was a little older than me, and he lived in Berlin. We wrote regularly to each other and became good friends. He sent me a photograph of himself with one of his letters. I thought he was very dishy, and I sometimes wondered if we would ever meet.

Werner

He would only write in German and I would reply clumsily in this new language. We wrote back and forth for some years, talking about books and music, but in 1939 I received the last letter he would send me.

His letter arrived on September 7th and it told me that he had been forced to join the German army, like every German man over the age of eighteen. He had been assigned to the Infantry as a foot soldier. I could not understand it, as by then he had qualified as a dentist and would surely have been given a higher rank. One month later it was announced that Britain was at war with Germany. My school boyfriend, George, had also been drafted by the British Army. I tried not to wonder if he and Werner would ever meet.

Adolf Hitler

It was during my German lessons at school that I first began to hear about a man called Adolf Hitler. Hitler was born in a small Austrian town in 1889, but as a teenager moved to the capital city, Vienna, close to a Jewish community. Although nobody knows what caused it, he developed a hatred of Jewish people that would go on to change the lives of so many, not only in Germany but across Britain and the whole of Europe too.

Hitler began his working life in Vienna as an artist, but was unsuccessful. He sold very few paintings, certainly not enough to make a living.

Hitler became bitter and left Austria in 1913, moving to Germany when he was a young man of twenty-four. When the First World War began in 1914, although still an Austrian citizen, he joined the German army and became a corporal; quite a low position which meant working as a runner and delivering messages on the Western Front. Not much is known of his activities, but he must have done well because he received a medal for his efforts and was later promoted to a junior officer.

At the end of that war, which lasted until 1918, the Treaty of Versailles was signed. Germany was told how many people they could have in their army, and what weapons they were allowed. The land they had taken over had to be given back, and demands were made for repayment for the damage caused to other countries where fighting had taken place. A huge amount of over six billion pounds was paid in gold, ships, and other things. One special condition to protect France was that the Rhineland, the German area on the borders of France, was to be called a demilitarised zone, which meant that no German forces or weapons were allowed in that area. This made Hitler angry, as he felt this treaty dishonoured Germany, and he promised that he would make the country great again.

This was the beginning of his rise to power. After the First World War he joined a political party called the German Workers' Party, which held anti-communist, anti-semitic (this means that they hated the Jews), and extreme nationalist beliefs. He gradually gained more influence, and he became known as the party's strongest and most important public speaker, persuading his followers that all the problems the Germans were suffering from after the war were caused by the Jews and the Communists.

An important moment in the story came just over two months after I was born in 1921. Two years after joining, Hitler left the DAP, announcing that he would only rejoin if he was made party chairman. Given his impressive influence, the party gave him what he wanted, and he replaced Anton Dexler as the leader of the now-named National Socialist German Workers' Party, known to the rest of the world as the Nazi Party.

The Swastika flag

From then on, Hitler's power only seemed to grow stronger and stronger. After requesting position of

Chancellor of the Nazi-Nationalist government in 1932 and being refused, he was finally given the job the following year. Now he was able to make decisions and act without the permission of parliament or being limited by laws. The only person whose power Hitler's didn't overrule was the German president, Paul von Hindenburg, who had been trying to tame Hitler for years. But when Hindenburg died in 1934, Hitler took the power of the president as well as the power he already had as chancellor, and named himself *'der Führer'* (German for leader).

Everything changed.

Hitler used his new power to bring in laws to punish the Jews, and his followers learned to hate them too. Shops and businesses with Jewish owners were broken into and ransacked. The homes of Jewish families were vandalised and damaged, their front doors branded with the ugly scraw *'Juden'*, the German word for 'Jews'. People were terrified. The Jewish population of Germany realised that they would surely be imprisoned or even killed by Hitler's secret police, the Gestapo. This was the beginning of what we now call the Holocaust.

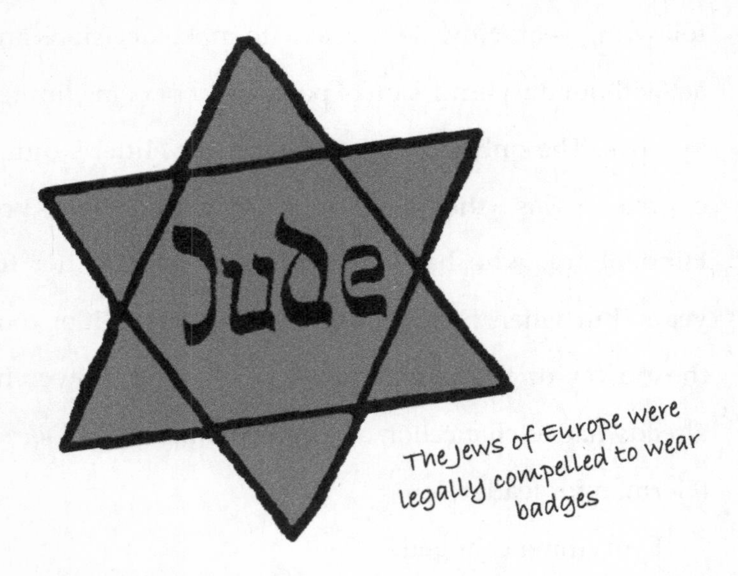

Jude
The Jews of Europe were legally compelled to wear badges

Many tried to leave Germany, but only those with plenty of money were able to escape, and they travelled to Britain or the United States if they could.

Those who were unable to escape ended up in death camps. The most famous of these camps today are Auschwitz and Treblinka, but there were many more of these awful places in Germany and Poland. In every one cruelty and death ruled supreme.

*

None of us realised how this terrible man would affect the lives of millions of people, but in the years to come we began to fear that perhaps there might be another war. My parents' generation had already suffered throughout the First World War. I couldn't understand how this man had become so powerful, or why the German population were following him with such blind adoration.

I remember when I first saw his photograph I could not believe it. He was quite a small man, with a funny little moustache and a strange, combed-over hairstyle.

People said that he would greet people by raising his right arm and saying, '*Heil*'. They would immediately raise their arm in return and shout out '*Heil Hitler*!' This German word means 'Hail' and is used as a greeting. It had to be used always by civilians, no more shaking hands or saying hello. The arm had to be raised exactly to an angle of forty-five degrees. If you were a soldier or were in the Gestapo, Hitler's secret police, you had to click your heels as well. Imagine what they looked like!

I always thought that it must have looked rather silly.

We used to see news films in the cinema that showed meetings in enormous halls where Hitler would be speaking. Everyone there would be standing with their arms raised at this special angle and shouting out the words, '*Heil Hitler*!' He was like a god to some. In many countries it is forbidden to use the greeting, '*Heil Hitler*' and even '*Sieg Heil*', meaning 'hail to victory' to this day as it represents such terrible, terrible memories for many people.

Years later, after the war was over and peace was declared in 1945, my mother wrote to tell me she had received a letter from the mother of my German pen-friend. She sent me the letter, written in German, which by then I was able to translate with ease.

Werner had died in 1940. He was killed at Arras in France in the early days of the war. His mother bitterly wrote that he had been placed on the front line as 'cannon fodder', positioned with other men who weren't worth protecting in the eyes of the German army. I was very confused; Werner had been from a good family, a qualified dentist, an important person.

Years after receiving my last letter from Werner, I went to Germany to meet his sister, Gea. She told me the terrible story. When Hitler took to power as *'der Führer'*, the German population was subjected to thorough checks. Any person with any Jewish blood in their family line, even a distant great-grandparent, was labelled 'a second class citizen' just as the other Jewish families in German were treated as such. They were forced to wear a yellow, fabric star on their clothes. As a second class citizen, it was no surprise that Werner had been put in the front line of the infantry as the first target for the enemy.

Only Werner and Gea's great-grandmother had been Jewish. Gea had suffered during the war as well. She had been sent to Auschwitz; not as a prisoner, but as a worker. She was given a simple but awful job. She was forced to keep a list of all the items that the German soldiers took from the Jews as they arrived in the camp: coins, books, toys, shoes, clothes. She knew that every person whose possessions she wrote down would soon be gassed.

Even after the war, Gea never married. The only men she met when she was a young girl were the cruel guards in the camp, and so she decided she would prefer to live her life alone.

I still have Werner's letters from all those years ago and sometimes when I read them I wonder what kind of life he would have had. Would he have still been a dentist, would he have had a family and a lovely big house? I truly wish I could have met him before the war.

CHAPTER THREE

Our lives were simple, but we still had lots of fun when we were teenagers. I was in the Girl Guides and played for the school hockey team. I used to go roller skating with my school friends, boys and girls, and loved it.

We played board games like Monopoly or draughts, and sometimes went camping. There were very few cars on the road then, so we would walk, take a bus or cycle everywhere. Romance was beginning to become a part of our lives too. My friends and I had crushes on film stars, and eventually we would fall in love.

I met my school boyfriend, George, when I was fourteen. George was tall and blond and very handsome, with just a trace of an attractive Scottish accent, and I adored him. We went everywhere together until we both left school. George's father, a police inspector, was relocated to Staines nearly thirty miles away. There were no mobile phones then, and we didn't have our own telephone in our house. George and I would arrange to phone from nearby public telephone boxes, and we wrote lots of letters to each another.

Television was only in its early beginnings. The first television broadcast was from a scruffy studio in Alexandra Palace in north London (or Ally Pally as we used to call it) on November 2nd 1936, when I was just fifteen. The British Broadcasting Corporation (BBC) rented a filthy little area in the eastern part of the palace, from which the first public television transmissions were made. One of the first engineers to work there described it as so disgusting that they could barely breathe inside, and had to hold their noses the entire time as they were trying to clean it up!

Only people who lived close enough to Ally Pally were able to get the broadcast. My family did live near enough, as Winchmore Hill was only a few miles away, but a television set was very expensive then so very few people could afford to buy one.

Luckily, a school friend's father had made a lot of money selling a medicine called 'Dr Williams' Pink Pills for Pale People' which were very popular with people who thought they would put more colour in their cheeks. He went straight out and bought his television set in the first

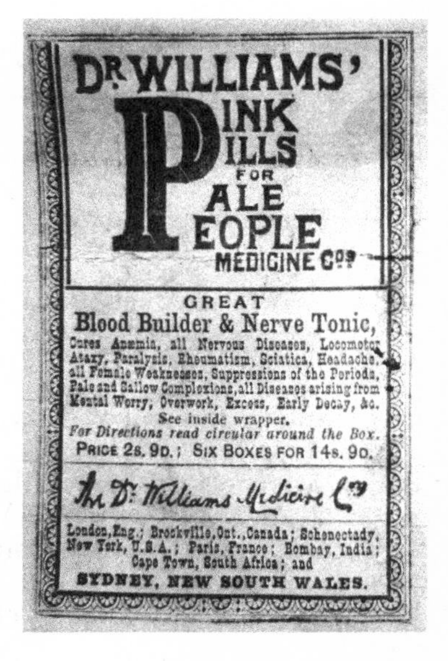

week. It was much more primitive than the ones you have now, but back then it was considered a marvel! My friend Doreen and I were invited to go and watch a programme there one evening, a broadcast of a football match.

There was no choice: a few American cartoons, a lot of sport and a few plays relayed from London theatres. Every afternoon they would show a dance band. The most famous one, which I can still remember, was Henry Hall and the BBC Dance Orchestra.

I expect your parents will watch the news on the

television at the same time every day, but we had to wait until 1954 before we could do that. We relied on the radio from our old wireless sets to learn what was going on in the world, or went to buy a newspaper from the local shop (we had never heard of supermarkets back then). Programmes were only shown for few hours a day, not twenty-four hours like people enjoy now. Even so, there were very few people who were able to watch it, and nobody ever thought it would be as popular as the wireless.

When war was imminent in 1939, television was taken off the air from September 1st. People were afraid that enemy bombers could lock onto the signal and use it as a guide to finding London. The last programme shown was a Mickey Mouse cartoon, which stopped half way through. When broadcasting returned in 1946 the BBC carried on with the same cartoon, from exactly the same place they had stopped it.

Ally Pally was used for secret operations to intercept the German radio navigation system towards the end of

1940. Special crews of the Luftwaffe, the German air force, were flying along beams which guided them to their target of central London. What we were able to do from Alexandra Palace was to bend the beams so that the enemy pilots lost their way and missed their target. This method managed to save a lot of lives.

Most children left school at fourteen in those days, unless we passed what we called the Scholarship Exam at the age of eleven. This allowed us to go to a Grammar School, where we stayed on until we were at least sixteen and when we would do our Matriculation Exams. I was lucky and passed the Scholarship Exam, and went on to an amazing secondary school, Southgate County.

The headmaster at Southgate was very unusual; on our first day he announced that we would take our Matriculation Exams, similar to A levels, after four years, rather than five years as most other schools did. He said we would then have the fifth year to begin our "real" education before we left school. We could choose from

Arts, Science or Commerce. Commerce meant anything to do with business; shorthand and typing, keeping accounts, understanding how banks worked and knowing something about company laws. After passing my Matriculation Exams I chose to study Commerce, and those skills have been incredibly useful to me ever since.

I would have loved to have gone on to university, but my parents couldn't afford it. As soon as I left school, I had to get a job as soon as possible. Luckily within two weeks of leaving school, just three weeks after my sixteenth birthday, I was working in the City of London for an insurance company, the Scottish Provident Assurance Company.

CHAPTER FOUR

What a change!

Every day I had to travel by steam train to Moorgate and then get the Tube. It was a mile walk to reach the office, right through the heart of the City of London – the Square Mile as it was called. I passed the Stock Exchange, the Mansion House where the Lord Mayor of London lived, and the Bank of England. I was surrounded by crowds of busy people with important jobs, who were all much older than me! It was quite a challenge.

In those days, women were considered inferior to men. I will never forget that first day when I arrived at the main London branch of the Scottish Provident Assurance Company at 3 Lombard Street. As I walked through the imposing front entrance, a young man about the same age as me arrived; he was also beginning his first day. We were both dressed to impress, and together we were taken to our department.

He was told to report straight away to the department manager, a man named Mr Mitcham, but I was called aside and told to go off with an older woman to collect an overall that would be my uniform. I can remember it to this day – it was a horrible purple hairy creation! Every female employee there had to wear it, even the general manager's secretary.

That was the first time I experienced different treatment to men, just because I was a girl. I had been to a mixed school where boys and girls were treated exactly the same, but I soon found out this would be the first occasion of many. I realised I had a fight on my hands to prove myself to be equal to my male colleagues, hopefully even better.

For a while it seemed I would work in the City for many years to come. I had been working there for about eight months, and I soon got to know the back lanes and interesting and historic places in the area during my lunchtime wanderings as I ate my homemade sandwiches (I didn't earn enough to buy lunch out).

Sometimes I would see important people arriving at the enormous Mansion House next door to our office, all coming to visit the Lord Mayor of London.

Out of the blue, my life experienced a big change, a total surprise. It was 1938, just before my seventeenth birthday. My life up to then had seemed quite ordinary. Isn't it funny how one letter can change everything?

That letter was from Mr Groves, my French and German teacher from school. He had written to my parents, telling them that he was giving up teaching to start the School Travel Service, a scheme to take groups of school children to visit other countries in Europe. He asked them if they would allow me to come and work for him.

I was over the moon! Travelling the world seemed much more interesting to me than working in an office with people so much older than I was.

Mr Groves said that I would have to spend some time working in France and Germany to polish up my language skills, and then he would employ me as a researcher. This would mean that I would travel round Europe to find suitable families in France and Germany where British school children could stay for a month to help improve *their* language skills. It sounded so exciting and I was all for it – imagine, travelling Europe at seventeen!

My parents were worried but finally I persuaded them that they could trust me to cope with such a change. Eventually my father said 'just go for it' and my mother conceded that I should 'follow my heart'. Of course, we had to find somewhere where I could go to start my studies, but also work to earn my keep. Searching in *The Lady*, we came across an advert from a family in a town called Contrexéville in the Vosges Mountains in France. I looked it up on the map and found it was on the eastern border of Germany, with the River Rhine separating the two countries.

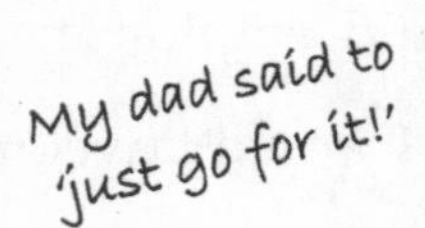

My dad said to
'just go for it!'

The family wanted an *au pair*; someone to teach their children English, who would also live as one of the family. There would be no wages, but I would be given a room and they would provide me with pocket money.

It sounded perfect.

We contacted them and said *'Oui'* without any hesitation. I sent references to show I was of good character and the reply came back right away saying they would be happy for me to join them. They sent the money to pay for my train and boat fares. How soon could I go? I wanted to get there as soon as possible! The only cloud hanging over me was the knowledge that I certainly would not see George again for a long time.

I handed in my notice to the Scottish Provident, and I was on my way in two weeks. Looking back, I had no idea what I was letting myself in for, but I hoped for the best. No more early morning struggles to find a seat on the train, no more having a quick sandwich on a bench outside the Royal Exchange, and no more having to wear a scratchy purple overall in the front office when all the men were wearing beautiful suits and ties. I bought a few extra clothes and a new suitcase and took £5, a fortune in those days, from my post office account. I was ready.

The letter I had received from France was written by Monsieur Marcel Boucher and was written on expensive looking notepaper. I realised that I was going to work for a French Member of Parliament. I was told there were three children: a five-year-old girl named Helène and two boys, eight-year-old Francois and ten-year-old Jean. I hoped I could cope with such a challenge – a new country and a new language to live with.

Francois, Jean & Helène

CHAPTER FIVE

It was a lovely day in May when I set out on my new adventure, first by train to the port of Dover and then by boat across the English Channel to Calais, where I took the train to Paris. It was the first time I had travelled that far without my parents and I was very anxious not to lose my luggage, holding on to it tightly throughout the journey. Another change and finally I was on the last leg of my trip. It was a long journey and I was alone, nobody spoke to me the whole way. Everyone seemed too occupied with their own affairs. Already I began to feel homesick.

Arriving at Contrexéville station, I found a large black Mercedes with a uniformed chauffeur and a very elegant lady who I presumed was Madame Boucher. I carefully tested out my French on her, and was relieved to see that she could understand me.

'You are the English girl?' she asked.

'Oui, Madame.'

As we made our way through the beautiful spa town, full of parks and flowers, she told me about her children and her husband.

Monsieur Boucher was a Minister of the French Parliament for the region of Vosges, and his wife told me he was always very busy and had to entertain a lot of visitors. Then

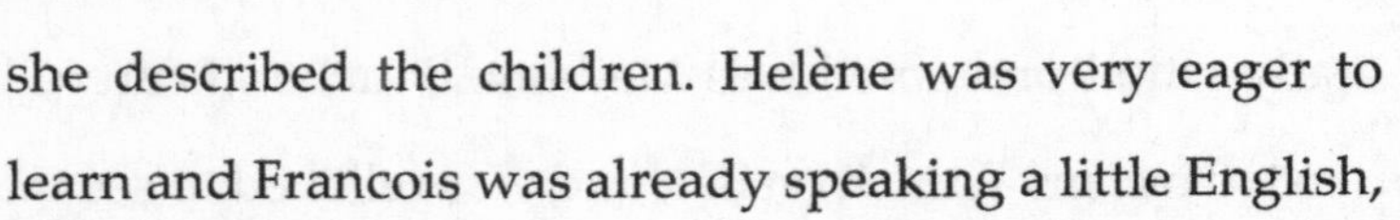

she described the children. Helène was very eager to learn and Francois was already speaking a little English, but then came Jean, the eldest. Madame Boucher smiled and said, 'He doesn't like learning things; he would rather be in the garden playing football.'

By then we had arrived at the entrance of a large house. It looked enormous compared to my house in Winchmore Hill; there was a long drive through a tree-lined avenue, the front door had two tall pillars either side, and the house was surrounded by a huge garden. As we drove through the gates, I wondered how I would fit in with such a rich and elegant background. How would I manage at meal times? Did they eat the same food? Were my clothes okay? I gritted my teeth and put my best foot forward.

Madame showed me my bedroom on the first floor and left me to settle in. It was a much bigger room than my humble bedroom at Winchmore Hill, large and sunny and overlooking the beautiful garden. Even the furniture was oversized, as if it grew to fill the space. My small collection of newly bought clothes looked lonely in the cavernous wardrobe.

My time was soon filled with so many new experiences that before long all my worries disappeared.

The children were very welcoming. After a few days, I found that they were very keen to learn English properly and make their parents proud of them. Although I had never taught before, I was enjoying every minute of it.

Every day the children would spend the mornings having their main lessons like Maths, Geography and History. Those teachers lived in the house as well, but they stayed in an apartment and had their meals there too. I didn't see much of them.

While the children were busy in the mornings, I wandered into the town or walked through the beautiful countryside. In the afternoon I would give the children their formal English lesson, followed by reading for around two hours, and then take them out to the woods, the park or the swimming pool. We made bows and arrows from tree branches we found, and played games such as Hide and Seek.

We would have breakfast and lunch together, and I would have dinner with their parents and any guests who were visiting.

It was like a banquet every evening. Can you imagine – an enormous table with a beautiful white tablecloth, with lots of different knives and forks on it, all for different dishes? There were three glasses, one for each wine that was served, and even I was offered a glass.

The two waiters who served our meals had long white aprons and always wore white gloves. Dinner seemed to go on and on and on. There were always interesting visitors coming to talk to the minister. I had to speak to them in my hesitant French, but it was improving every day. Sometimes the guests had important political connections, sometimes they were businessmen and often foreigners themselves struggling with their own French.

On one occasion the Romanian prime minister arrived – his French was definitely worse than mine!

It meant that I matured very quickly, not only meeting so many different and important people but also learning to understand the French menus and the delicious, but often unusual, dishes they served.

I remember one dessert in particular called *Croquembouche,* which means 'crunches in the mouth'. It was a tall thing, made of small round cream pastries piled into a pyramid and covered in caramel. That was only for special occasions. Everything was going well and I was happy in Contrexéville, until one day at the end of August.

As well as a politician, Monsieur Boucher was a part-time soldier, just like our Territorial Army. He had left to attend their annual camp near Strasbourg. They were camped on the banks of the River Rhine and on the other side of the river was Germany.

Monsieur Boucher had only been gone a day when I was called into the Madame's study and told to sit down. She looked very serious.

'You have to go home immediately,' she said.

I was gobsmacked. I thought I must have done something wrong. 'Why, what have I done?' I asked.

She put her arm around me. 'No, my dear, it is not you. It is the German army; Monsieur has telephoned to say they are camped on the other side of the river with their tanks. There is going to be a war.'

She explained that despite being forbidden, Hitler had now given orders to his troops to move into the Rhineland.

Madame could see how upset I was, far away from home and in a strange country. She tried to reassure me, but also make me understand how urgent it was that I should leave as soon as possible. Could I get home in time before war started or would I be left in France, stranded on my own?

'You must leave right away. We are too near the German border to take any risks. I'm sorry but it is much too dangerous.'

My dream was fading.

'Come,' she said. 'We must get your bags packed now. You must leave tomorrow as early as possible.'

CHAPTER SIX

The train to Paris was crowded. The floor of every carriage I looked in was piled high with luggage, not only suitcases but bundles of belongings wrapped in sheets, curtains, anything to keep them together. I thought I would never find an empty seat. Finally I came across one in the last carriage – it must have been the only one left. As I sat there, wondering what the future held, I realised the people around me were talking in a language which was neither French nor English. I tried to listen to what they were saying, but I couldn't make sense of it. It sounded a bit like German, but not quite. And then it came to me – it was Yiddish, the language the Jewish people used.

I realised that they must also be getting away from Germany before something terrible happened to them.

Looking in their faces, I could see how anxious and terrified they were.

Arriving in Paris, it was too late to get a train that night to Calais, so I had to find somewhere to stay. I didn't know what I was going to do. I had hardly any money and I didn't know Paris at all. I decided to find a policeman or *gendarme* as they are called in France. I was lucky. The policeman I found was very helpful and took me to a rest centre run by nuns, where I shared a small room with one of the sisters for the night.

I woke early the next morning. After a breakfast of croissants and coffee, I went to the *Gare du Nord* and took the first train to the coast so that I could get the ferry to Dover. Many of the same Jewish families from the day before were travelling on to Britain as well.

As the White Cliffs came in sight, anxious expressions soften into relieved smiles. Some delved into their bags, fishing out their precious jewellery, such as rings, bracelets and ornate tie pins. It occurred to me that they would probably have to sell these treasures later to help them settle into their new country, but for now I felt happy that they would at least be safe.

Exhausted but thankful to be home and safe again with my family, I had to decide what was next. I needed a new job, and soon I was working in another office for another company in London – but it was just as boring. Still, it was great to see my old friends again and go roller-skating at Ally Pally.

Many of my friends said that they were going to join the army. George would be going into the Military Police, following his father's footsteps. It seemed everyone expected we would soon be at war with Germany again. It was frightening to think about it.

By now Hitler had taken over Austria and invaded the northern and western parts of Czechoslovakia. It was becoming obvious that he would not stop there.

Neville Chamberlain, the British prime minister, knew that we were not strong enough to face another war. We didn't have enough trained soldiers or aeroplanes, and only our Navy was fit to fight. Things were desperate – we needed to stall for some time. A meeting was arranged with Hitler in September to try to avoid a war.

After a lot of talking, a compromise was agreed. This became known as the Munich Agreement. Hitler was allowed to take over the German-speaking parts of Czechoslovakia, which were given a new name, Sudetenland. The agreement was signed on September 30th 1938 and we all breathed a sigh of relief. The prime minister arrived home, and as he left the aeroplane he waved the agreement above his head, smiling. He made a speech that assured us of 'peace in our time'.

I still remember that day.

The whole family was sitting in front of the wireless. As we listened to the news, we truly believed him. I was incredibly relieved that George would not have to fight and risk getting injured or even killed.

CHAPTER SEVEN

Life went on as usual. Months passed and Christmas came and went. By the next summer all seemed calm, so I decided to visit Germany, and I booked a trip to Bonn on the border between France and Germany.

Arriving in Germany, I was shocked at what I found. We were greeted on the train by armed German police who demanded to search our luggage. My copy of the magazine '*Picture Post*' was confiscated. I was told it was forbidden. There were lots of armed soldiers in the streets and I saw many empty shops with the word '*Juden*' written on the windows.

Everywhere I went people were greeting one another with the '*Heil Hitler*' salute, and so one day as I went to buy some fruit I thought I would try it out. I was staying with a friend of my old school German teacher, and one of the girls came with me. As we entered the shop I raised my arm in a smart British Army salute and said, 'God save the King!', and brightly added, *'Apfel bitte!'* I wanted some apples.

Somebody gasped. The other shoppers didn't see the joke, and instead of laughing they glanced around anxiously with terrified faces. I realise now that they thought the Gestapo might have heard me and taken it as an insult. I remembered the armed police at the train station, and decided I should be more careful.

I returned home on August 25th 1939. Just over a week later we would be at war.

CHAPTER EIGHT

It was on September 1st 1939 when Hitler went back on his promise and invaded Poland. Life changed for all of us. Britain had signed an agreement to support Poland if the country was threatened. Now it had happened, and we had to honour our promise to our ally. On September 3rd there was an announcement that the prime minister would be making a broadcast.

That morning my family and I gathered around the radio to hear the news. My parents looked sick with worry and my brother and I were anxious too. My father was in his working clothes having just repaired a broken cupboard door, and my mother had joined us after preparing the vegetables for our usual Sunday lunch.

At 11.15am the prime minister said to the entire nation:

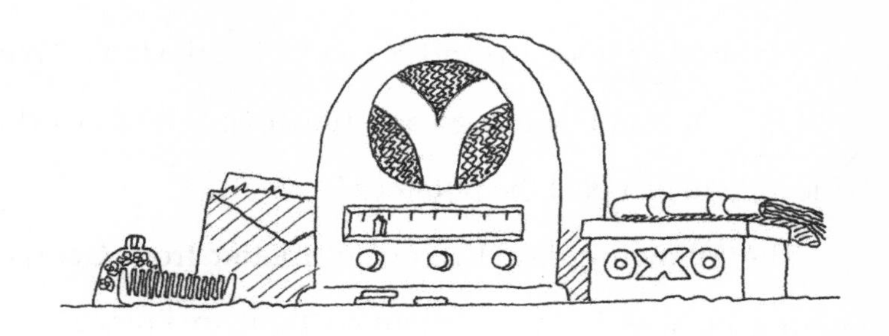

'This morning the British Ambassador in Berlin handed the German Government a final note stating that, unless we heard from them by eleven o'clock that they were prepared at once to withdraw their troops from Poland, a state of war would exist between us. I have to tell you now that no such undertaking has been received, and that consequently this country is at war with Germany.'

We looked at each other, wondering what this would mean. My father was the first to speak. 'Well, we're in for a hard time. I remember what it was like last time, and the Germans have many more aeroplanes now. We'll be bombed here in London, you take my word.' He sighed.

My mother stood up and began laying the table. 'We still have to eat. Dennis, go and finish your homework. Eileen, you can peel the potatoes.'

The following day, I received a letter from George saying he was leaving Britain to fight in France. We hadn't seen each other for weeks. George was in military training and now, with weeks of silence in front of me, I wondered if I would ever get to see him again.

Realising that war was inevitable, the British Government had been quietly preparing. They had predicted that Hitler would continue moving into all the territory he wanted, but the Munich Agreement had given them time to prepare their resources and they had become stronger. They were able to train more soldiers and build more aircraft. They also realised that Britain would quickly become a target for bombers, and they had prepared for this too.

In no time, every home in London was issued with air raid shelters. When our shelter arrived at Winchmore Hill, it was simply a pile of large corrugated iron sheets that we had to put together ourselves. My mother, father, Dennis and I dug a hole in the garden big enough to take the shelter and erected it bit by bit.

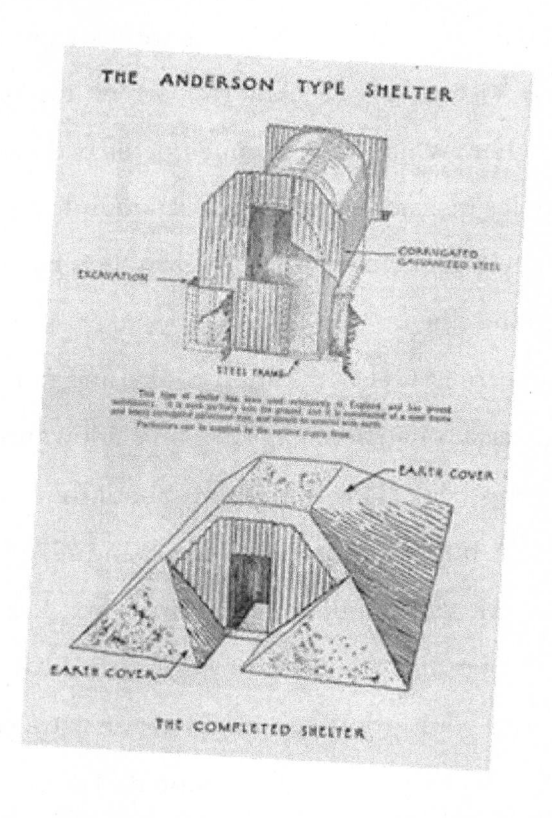

All the soil was piled on the shelter's roof, and we were instructed to plant grass on top so that it could not be seen from the air.

The Government started rationing food in January 1940; a result of the ships which carried such foods as oranges, bananas, sugar and meat, being a prime target for the enemy. Those of us with gardens were asked to 'Dig for Victory' so we grew rhubarb on top of our air raid shelter. We all dug up our flower beds and grew vegetables instead just to give us enough to eat. People kept rabbits and chickens and pigs in their back garden, even in the cities.

We were issued with ration books, and families had to register at one shop. One person's allowance would be one fresh egg, 113g margarine, about four rashers of bacon, 57g butter and tea, 28g cheese, and 227g sugar for a week. Meat was allocated by price, so cheaper cuts became popular, but if you were friends with your butcher or your grocer you might get an extra couple of sausages secretly 'under the counter'. The shopkeeper would cut the coupons out of your ration book as they gave you the items. Points could be pooled or saved to buy cereals, tinned goods, dried fruit, biscuits and jam.

Sweets were rationed from 1942, and this went on for nine years after the war . Carrots replaced sugar in apple tarts and we even ate them on sticks as lollies!

If you wanted to eat in a restaurant, the meal had to cost no more than five shillings – that is only twenty-five pence in today's money – but people only earned around £2 to £5 a week then. When you went on holiday to a hotel for more than three days you had to give up ration coupons.

Other items like petrol were rationed too, but you were only issued with petrol coupons if you owned a business, or for medical reasons. We were even given clothes coupons, and styles became very simple. Men's trousers had no turn-ups and women's clothing became a lot more practical. Ruffles and pleats disappeared, as did brightly coloured fabrics. Girls even started painting gravy browning on their legs to look like stockings!

Not all rationing finished at the end of the war. It would not be until January 1950 that petrol rationing ceased, five years after the war ended, and some foods were rationed right up until 1954.

Meanwhile in 1939, every day and night for months we wondered when the Luftwaffe bombings would begin.

CHAPTER NINE

George had gone with the British Expeditionary Force, the new name given to our soldiers who had been sent to France to support our allies immediately after war was declared. They joined the French troops on the border with Belgium at the Maginot Line, a defence built by France to protect its borders. They waited for the Germans to attack, but for months nothing happened, as Germany was concentrating on invading Poland and Czechoslovakia. Every day we thought 'Jerry', our name for the enemy, would attack, but we waited and waited, and nothing happened. This lasted from September until the end of April the next year. We called this *The Phoney War*.

Hitler's troops quickly defeated any resistance in Holland and Belgium, moving and as far as the French border to the Maginot Line and setting up their own defence called the Siegfried Line.

It was not until May 10th 1940 that Hitler's troops went into action again. They soon overwhelmed the French forces and our own soldiers who were no match for Hitler's army. The Germans were better equipped and more experienced, having supported General Franco's troops in Spain in their civil war in 1936. The Allied troops were pushed farther and farther back through France. Many British soldiers were captured and many more killed. Their only option was to retreat. It was a disaster. Broken and defeated, the soldiers made their way as best they could towards the north coast of France, heading for the port of Dunkirk. Some were able to get a lift on salvaged cars or trucks

Franco

and even on farm tractors. Most had to march. They would join up in small groups and try to look like an army, but an army in retreat. Units of the French army tried to hold back the Nazi advance to allow as many Allied soldiers as possible to escape. Clutching sticks cut from the trees, with their arms in slings or their legs all bandaged, those who were injured stumbled on. They had little food, only what they could get from the villages they passed through or salvage from the fields.

Back in Winchmore Hill, we listened to the news, helplessly wondering how many would escape. All I could think of was whether George was safe.

The government released a public announcement pleading with anyone who owned a boat, large or small, to aid their soldiers. The response was incredible. Seven hundred fishing boats, life boats and paddle steamers, rowing boats and private yachts responded to the call and made their way over to the beaches. There they found our troops lying in the sand, tired and defeated.

None of us could have imagined that the lives of almost 340,000 of our soldiers would be saved by ordinary civilian craft. They are still known as the Little Ships of Dunkirk, and each year they re-assemble and go back to remember those amazing, terrifying days.

Can you imagine the surprise and relief of these soldiers, who thought they would be killed in the bombings or taken as prisoners, when they saw these little ships coming to rescue them? The men on the beaches waded as far as they could into the sea, some up to their necks in the water, hoping to be picked up. They climbed aboard the ships and were ferried out to the larger Navy and passenger vessels, while all the time the German Stuka aircraft were dive-bombing them. Many boats were sunk, their cargoes of soldiers trying to keep afloat in the sea, hoping to survive. A lot more landed safely at the various south coast ports. It was a disaster which became a victory.

Those of us at home would listen to the news all day, wondering and worrying about our family and friends.

Had they been saved? Would they return? I tried not to think about where George might be.

We lost 68,000 soldiers in the campaign and almost all of our tanks and other equipment. But we saved almost 350,000 of our troops at Dunkirk. At the time, we wondered whether we would survive. In the event we felt it was our finest hour.

CHAPTER TEN

By this point, many London-based companies had realised they were likely to be a target if Hitler started bombing our cities. Already a large number of them had evacuated their offices away from the capital, many schools in London had moved away to somewhere safer, and children as young as five or six were separated from their parents and sent miles away to live in the country with people they did not know, where they would be safe. The railway stations were filled with children waiting for the trains to take them away, their parents crying on the

EVACUATION
OF
WOMEN AND CHILDREN
FROM LONDON, Etc.

FRIDAY, 1st SEPTEMBER.
Up and Down business trains as usual with few exceptions.
Main Line and Suburban services will be curtailed while evacuation is in progress during the day.

SATURDAY & SUNDAY,
SEPTEMBER 2nd & 3rd.
The train service will be exactly the same as on Friday.
Remember that there will be very few Down Mid-day business trains on Saturday.

SOUTHERN RAILWAY

platform. Every child was labelled with their name, and when they arrived at their destination new families were waiting to choose those they wanted. There would always be a couple left until last. Imagine how you'd feel if that was you?

In April I received a letter from the Scottish Provident Institution. It read: *'Dear Miss le Croissette, We would like to offer you a post back with our company...'*

A lot of the men who worked there had been called up to join the Army, and they needed women to take their places. The Scottish Provident had moved their offices to Surrey, convinced that London would be the first target for the German bombers. I decided to set off for Woking.

We all lived together in a big house on the outskirts of the town. I was given an enormous bedroom with a double bed. I hadn't even had a double bed while I was staying with the Bouchers in France! We lived together and worked together, there was no escaping the other people. I was getting very bored. I was the only teenager there by then, as all the young men had been called up to join the Army, Navy or the Air Force. All the older women spent their evenings smoking and drinking, and talking about work and their families. I decided to find something else more useful – and maybe fun – to do in my spare time.

Near Woking there was the Inkerman Barracks where the new soldiers were trained before they were sent to France. They would spend their free time in the canteen of the YMCA, and the organisers were always looking for volunteers to help there, so I decided to join them.

Most of the soldiers were young and had never left home before; a lot came from Scotland, all with a very strong accent. We would try to make their time off a little more interesting. We were always busy but we had a lot of fun and often went out with the soldiers, although we couldn't get too attached. They would be there one evening and then on their way overseas the next day. I still have a photo of one of them. I often wonder if he survived.

*

As soon as the Dunkirk evacuation began, everything changed. Because so many troops were arriving at the south coast, it was impossible to feed them as they arrived at the ports. The ones who were badly injured were taken to hospital and the rest were put on the next train to wherever it was going. The first large station was asked to provide refreshments for them. Woking was one of their first stops. Immediately, the Services canteen was moved on to the station platform.

For nine days the canteen was open twenty-four hours a day to offer hot drinks, sandwiches and sometimes cakes as the trains drew in. The train remained there for only ten minutes. Realising that these troops needed all the support they could be given after such a terrible time, I was given permission by the office manager to work at the train station full-time for as long as I was needed. People made hundreds of sandwiches and cakes using their own food rations. Huge pots of hot soup were brought out and the tea urns were always full.

It was an experience I will always remember.

The survivors from Dunkirk arrived with their uniforms torn, filthy and sometimes covered in blood. Their faces were grey with tiredness and hunger, but when they had their mug of tea and their sandwiches they would smile and say thank you and then climb back onto the train to face whatever their future held. Every day I would look to see if there was anyone I knew who had escaped. I often wondered about George.

On the third day I noticed someone getting out of the carriage right opposite my serving station who seemed to have a different uniform from the others. His grey trousers caught my eye; no British Army khaki or Air Force blue.

He came towards me looking for a mug of tea, and as he noticed me his face lit up and he exclaimed in French: 'My God, it's Eileen!'

I looked up in surprise. René Cadier stood in front of me, wearing the uniform of the French Air Force with pilot wings pinned on his chest.

René's badge

I had met René when I was at school. He'd visited with a group of French students and we became good friends; we even exchanged the odd letter after he returned home.

We were so surprised and happy to see one another!

René told me how he had joined the French Air Force before the war began and had trained as a fighter pilot. A week earlier his plane had been shot down but he had managed to parachute out and wasn't too badly injured. He had no choice but to walk alone for several miles, finally meeting up with a group of British soldiers making their way to the coast. And here he was, battered and exhausted, but safe.

René hardly had time to gulp down his tea before he had to get back on the train. I gave him my new address and telephone number, along with an extra pack of sandwiches, and he promised to let me know where he landed up. It was incredible that he had arrived at the very time I was on duty and opposite where I was working – just another of life's strange coincidences.

More than a month later, I received a letter. My heart raced as I recognised George's handwriting on the envelope; my relief was enormous. I knew that he was safe, but it would be years until I would find out how he had escaped.

George was one of many heroes of the Dunkirk Evacuation. He deserved a medal. As a military policeman, George had been sent to Dunkirk to patrol the beaches, as the soldiers were waiting to be rescued. They had to be taken in the boats out to the larger vessels off shore.

With his experience in rowing from his school days in the Staines Rowing Club, George realised he could help when he found an upturned boat on the shore. He got another man who could also row to join him and they took boatload after boatload of the desperate men out to the waiting vessels.

After nearly ten hours, an officer on one of the naval ships could see how exhausted they were and said, 'That's enough, no more. Jump aboard!' And George was saved. He was one of many heroes during the evacuation.

CHAPTER ELEVEN

A few weeks after Dunkirk, Hitler gave the orders that launched The Battle of Britain; the first battle in history to be waged only in the air.

I often saw the 'dogfights' in the skies above southern England as our Spitfires and Hurricanes took on the German bombers and their fighter escorts. Our pilots were generally outnumbered, but inflicted such heavy losses that Hitler abandoned his plans to invade. Britain was saved. Later, I would learn the secret of their success as I played my own part in the air war.

We had expected Germany to bomb the large British cities, but first the Luftwaffe attacked the ports on the south coast and the shipping convoys bringing food to our shores. He wanted to starve us out. Hitler then gave orders to bomb aircraft factories and anti-aircraft defences to pave the way for an invasion by his army. We were wondering where the next bomb would hit.

I always hoped for letters from George to arrive in the post, telling me that he was okay. I had only received a few short notes, always saying that he was thinking of me. The last letter just said: *'I am at a training camp before being sent overseas.'* I had heard that there was fighting in North Africa, and so I wondered if that's where he might go.

It was a time of great danger for Britain and, for Hitler, a time of vital importance. He knew that Germany's Air Force had to be stronger than Britain's to have an advantage in the war. His next move was to attack the British airfields, trying to destroy our fighter aircrafts. In London, you could hear the German planes – they sounded deeper than British planes.

Finally, our greatest fear was realised. The first bombs that fell on London on August 24th were an accident, meant for military grounds. Until now there had been no city attacks, but the Luftwaffe's targets were on the outskirts of the capital. Flying just slightly off course, a bomb hit the centre of London, killing hundreds of people and destroying many homes. My parents phoned me the next day and told me how they watched the fires blazing from the upstairs window at Winchmore Hill and listened to the clatter of anti-aircraft guns, wondering if it would be their turn next.

By this time, Neville Chamberlain had resigned and Winston Churchill had become the new British prime minister. Believing that the London attack was deliberate, Churchill fought back and ordered the British bombers to target Germany's capital, Berlin. Hitler had promised the German people that the capital would never become a target. When he realised this was no longer true, the

Commander of the Luftwaffe was given further orders: 'Our great *Furher* has vowed to obliterate the cities of Britain.'

And the Blitz began.

I was returning home from Woking for the weekend on September 7th, when 348 German bombers and 617 fighter planes darkened the London sky. As we got off the train at Paddington Station we could hear gunfire and see the shadowy silhouettes of the enemy planes in the sky above. Buildings were destroyed by lightning flashes as the German bombs hit and fires raged all over the city. Already we could see smoke and flames coming from the area around the Docks. Hundreds of terrified people were killed in their homes and many more left wounded. The British planes trying to fight back were outnumbered thanks to Hitler's earlier strikes, but they were able to use a new technique called 'Range and Direction Finding' (RDF), which gave them enough warning of incoming bombers to shoot them down. They were heroes.

The bombing continued until six o'clock in the

evening, but there was little time to rest before the Luftwaffe came back again for a second attack that same night, guided by the fires still burning below. Finally, at four o'clock in the morning, it seemed to be over.

For fifty-five days and nights it went on. Every day the scene would be different. Houses that were there yesterday would be gone today; sometimes the front of houses would be blown out. Riding past on the train, you could see the insides of people's homes. You might see their dining table all set ready for a meal, and nobody there.

Londoners who didn't have their own air raid shelters, or whose houses had already been destroyed, would make their way to the nearest tube station or underground shelter that they could find, as soon as they heard the air raid siren. Families would sleep in the tube stations for weeks on end. Sometimes the children couldn't go outside into the open air for days and their faces would be grey with lack of sleep. They had faces like old men. People could only wash in the basins in the station toilets. I can only imagine how awful it was. But still they would keep cheerful by singing all together, songs like *Roll Out the Barrel* and *There Will Always Be an England.* I think it was here that the real cockney spirit showed itself.

Other cities suffered bombings too, but nowhere near as often as London. Coventry was one of the cities to be hit worst; more people were killed in one night than anywhere else in the country. Hitler was aiming for the many factories there.

Hitler was trying to break Britain and make us give in, but we never did. We made up our minds to beat him in any way possible, and nobody dared to think we would lose. We had all lost friends and family in the air raids; many famous buildings were damaged or destroyed, even Buckingham Palace and the Houses of Parliament were hit. Although they sent their daughters away, King George and Queen Elizabeth insisted on staying at Buckingham Palace rather than moving to a safer location, even when a bomb landed in the grounds.

On June 4th 1940, Winston Churchill spoke the words, 'We shall fight on the beaches, we shall fight on the landing grounds, we shall fight in the fields and in the streets, we shall fight in the hills; we shall never surrender.' This speech is remembered to this day.

I remember returning home from Woking one weekend and, as we were arriving at Paddington Station, I was horrified to see hanging on the telephone lines a parachute bomb. The wind was catching the parachute slightly as it blew. I was worried that it would eventually fall and explode. I was relieved when we passed it safely.

Although the German Navy, *Kriegsmarine,* were ready and waiting on the coast of France to invade Britain, Hitler knew he would never be able to gain ground without defeating our Air Force. Their ships were clumsy, flat-bottomed barges, most of which needed to be towed, and they couldn't sail at all on rough sea.

As time went by, Germany lost more and more of its bombing force to Britain. Eventually, Hitler realised he would not manage to beat our Air Force and he knew our Navy was stronger than his. He decided to open a second front, a new battleground, by invading Russia, which was part of the Soviet Union.

On June 21st 1941 the German forces invaded. Initially they were very successful, conquering large areas of the country. Thousands of people were killed in those first few months. The enemy was advancing towards Moscow but the Soviet government fought back and the Battle of Stalingrad, from the winter of 1942 to 1943, was the turning point.

The Soviet army was used to the bitter winter weather, but the German soldiers weren't prepared for these harsh conditions. The Russians were regaining ground. Britain had learnt their lessons from Hitler's strategy and had begun targeting German factories in the Ruhr, halting the production of weapons, military uniforms and other vital equipment. Without these, the German fighters were at a big disadvantage, and would eventually be defeated.

*

We all were becoming more and more determined to join in the fight and beat the enemy. I can remember two older sisters living in our street would wait until we were given the All Clear, and then they would go out into the street, shaking their walking sticks at the sky and shouting: 'You won't beat us, you Nazis!'

Our food rations were becoming more and more limited, and my mother used to tell me how difficult it was to find something different to feed the family. We were already growing potatoes, Brussels sprouts, rhubarb and peas in our garden. The fishmongers had started to sell something called snoek and even whale meat, but people thought that whale was a bit oily. More and more, the meat ration was shrinking and butchers were selling offal – which really meant any of the bits of animals you wouldn't normally eat!

People had to make do, and the government was now sending out vitamins like cod liver oil to try and perk up the country's health. Meanwhile the bombings went on, but gradually our fighters were having more success.

CHAPTER TWELVE

In August 1940 I received some terrible news. My favourite cousin, who had trained to be a fighter pilot in the RAF, had been killed in a plane crash during a heavy summer storm. This prompted me to realise that working in an office, safely tucked away in Woking, I was doing nothing to help my country.

It was decided. I would volunteer for the Royal Air Force. I told my parents about my new ambition, and straight away my father said: 'Well, you're old enough to make up your own mind. Follow your heart, and we will always support you.' I sent off my application in November, and soon enough I received a reply telling me to report for an interview in January. I was just nineteen.

My interview date came closer, and the day before it arrived I bumped into an old school mate. She was already in the uniform of the Women's Auxiliary Air Force, and I thought how great she looked! I told her I was joining the WAAF and she gave me some advice.

'They are sure to ask you whether you want to be a cook or a driver,' she said. 'You tell them you want to be a *Clerk Special Duties.*'

'But what's that?' I asked.

'I can't tell you,' she replied, 'but just tell them you are good at maths.'

She would not tell me anything more. Surprised, I walked away desperately trying not to forget her advice.

The following day, at the interview in London, sure enough the rather terrifying-looking senior WAAF officer asked me, 'Which do you want to be – a cook or a driver?'

Feeling rather anxious, I repeated my friend's words. 'I want to be a *Clerk Special Duties.*' It was as if I had let off a bomb. Her eyes shot up to mine, and I thought she was going to hit the ceiling.

'What do you know about that?' she demanded.

Hesitantly I took a breath and replied, 'I don't know what it is, but I am good at maths.' These seemed to be the magic words, and she wrote on my form 'Recommended for Clerk Special Duties.' I was told to return home and wait for my calling-up papers. I would have a railway warrant and I would be sent to my first camp for initial training. I went back to Woking and gave in my notice. Then I returned home, wrote to George, telling him I was joining up, and waited to be called.

As time passed I wondered what I had let myself in for, but I knew I was doing the right thing. I knew that my call-up papers would be sent to my parents' address, and so I rang every evening when I finished work.

'Has it come yet?'

'No, dear. Not yet.'

Finally in March a letter arrived giving me instructions to report to the WAAF training camp at Innsworth, Gloucester, and a railway warrant for my train. I was excited now. I rushed to tell my manager the news that I would be leaving sooner than expected and I was given my final month's wages as well as an extra £2.

The next day I was back at home in Woking, starting to prepare for my next adventure. I packed my battered leather suitcase with a few underclothes, toiletries, notepaper and stamps; not much else except for a book to read on the train and a packet of Spam sandwiches.

On the morning of my journey my mother insisted that I ate a large breakfast, saying, 'You don't know when you'll have your next proper meal!' She then pressed a pound note into my hand. I knew that my father only earned £4 a week, and so I hastily tried to give it back. She looked at me seriously. 'You may need it,' she said, and kissed me goodbye. 'Hurry now; you mustn't miss your train!'

I made my way to the local railway station, passing the familiar shops I had known since I was a child – past the Little Lady's sweet shop, where I had once collected the cards from the penny bars of Nestle's chocolate I bought with my pocket money, past the village green. I was on my way to a new life.

The train from Paddington to Gloucester was crowded, mostly with soldiers and airmen, but I finally found a seat. Opposite me were two women wearing

WAAF uniform, also going to Gloucester. I sat pretending to read my book, quietly listening to them chatting. It seemed they were working in the offices there, dealing with the new entrants. Eventually I plucked up the courage to speak, 'I'm just on my way to join up. I'm going to RAF Innsworth.'

They both laughed and one said, 'You won't know what's hit you. Still, it only lasts a couple of weeks.'

On arriving at Gloucester, a large truck was waiting for us. It was already full of airmen. There were six other girls there, all looking nervous. After about fifteen minutes, the truck reached its last stop – an enormous camp.

I checked in and was sent to a Nissen hut and told to report to the corporal there.

'How do I know who is a corporal?' I asked, confused.

I didn't know anything about Air Force ranks, but I soon found out that a corporal would wear two stripes on her arm and a sergeant would have three.

In the hut, there were about thirty beds in two straight

lines against the walls and in the middle a metal stove with the chimney going up into the roof. The corporal, a tall and bossy girl with a strong northern accent, showed me to a spare bed. There was a sorry looking mat on the floor, a small cabinet by the bedside and a hook on the wall to hang up my uniform, and three square pads, solid and covered in itchy looking brown fabric, piled up, called *biscuits*.

'You put them together to make a mattress,' the corporal explained. She showed me how to make the bed with the brown blankets and a thin, limp pillow.

'But you can't do that until 1700 hours.'

'That's five o'clock,' I reminded myself. That was my introduction to the twenty-four hour clock, which I would use for the next six years.

'You will get up at 0600 hours and then make your bed. The ablutions are there.' She pointed to a door at the end of the hut, leading to the toilets and showers.

She then directed me to another large hut on the other side of the camp where I had to go to be fitted for my uniform – a jacket and a skirt, two air force blue shirts, a top coat and a khaki rubber groundsheet which was also to be used as a raincoat. I was given two pairs of heavy black shoes, two vests and two pairs of enormous black long-legged knickers we called 'blackouts'.

The final items were a sewing kit, a metal plate, a tin mug and a pack containing a knife, fork and spoon which they called my irons and were kept in a linen bag.

The corporal returned. 'Get cracking and line up outside – time for your medical and your FFI, and then your injections.'

'What on earth is that?' I asked.

'Free From Infection. We check you don't have nits, and if you do, we treat your hair with paraffin to kill them off!'

'Gawd 'elp us!' said one of the other girls. We looked around at each other, wondering who might have that humiliation.

CHAPTER THIRTEEN

We marched back to our hut, an unlikely group. By then the whole hut was full of girls, some as young as me, some much older, but all new recruits and wondering what they were going to do there. I soon found out what a mixture we were. My bed was between two girls who seemed to know each other quite well, called Peggy and Jean, both were from Devon.

One very quiet girl whispered her introduction, 'I'm Doreen and I'm from Southampton.' Then there was Nancy, a loud character who announced that she had decided to join up because she was fed up of men, and Hettie, a Cockney girl who was very friendly. We got on immediately, and began chatting right away. As I attempted to keep up with the others to return to the hut, I tried not to giggle as she whispered to me: 'You won't get me wearing those black bloomers!'

We all were called to tea at the Mess, which was thick corned-beef sandwiches, a slice of *yellow peril* – a solid rock of cake – and strong tea.

After the meal, and while the girls were trying on their uniforms and laughing at Hettie parading around in her blackouts, I managed to slip off to call my parents. I could only talk for a few minutes as there was a long queue forming behind me, but I just had time to ask my father to send me a bath plug.

'What on earth do you want that for? Are you going

to be a plumber?'

'No,' I explained. 'I have seen the baths and none of them have plugs in them, so I thought it would be a good idea if I had my own.' I could hear him laughing down the phone.

The following days were a jumble of marching in time, left right, left right, learning the ranks of officers, how to salute and who to salute. Then we were told the history of the RAF, how much leave we might get, how much pay we would get, what to do and what not to do, but I still didn't know anything about my role. I asked around what the others were hoping to be trained for. There were girls who would be trained as drivers and cooks, parachute packers and telephone operators, but no mention of Clerks Special Duties.

The two weeks of training flew by and my last day at Innsworth finally arrived. We were called in to the office one by one to find out where we would be posted. Finally, I was given another rail warrant and told to report to RAF Leighton Buzzard, where my special training would begin.

I stood with my RAF members for the pay parade and waited for my name to be called out – *'445020 le Croissette'* – and came forward to receive my pay. I was growing more and more excited – finally I would know what Clerk Special Duties meant! We spent our last night in hut seven packing the things we had brought from home, along with our uniforms, our irons, and our black bloomers.

CHAPTER FOURTEEN

I was allowed to go back home to Winchmore Hill for the weekend before I set off to Leighton Buzzard. My parents were delighted to see me in uniform for the first time, even if it was only a brief visit. Even Dennis said I looked smart! After two weeks of batch-cooked meals and slabs of dry cake, I was looking forward to some home cooking. My mother had presumably saved their precious rations for our Sunday lunch – her Yorkshire puddings must have used their egg ration for the month and their meat ration on the joint of beef. It was wonderful!

Later that evening, after a quiet train ride, I arrived at Leighton Buzzard with around thirteen other recruits. We reported as usual to the guardroom, and I noticed that unlike the simple base at Innsworth, everything here was covered in leafy camouflage. The buildings were concealed by a heavy green fabric with the outlines of trees painted on it, obviously trying to blend in with the countryside.

What was so important that it had to be hidden like this?

Once again, we were all shown to our beds in the dorms, in a building suspiciously called the Workhouse, and sent to report back to the main building. I found there were about twenty of us on the course, and we all assembled and waited for instructions.

A wing commander entered the room and began to speak. 'You have all been chosen for a special job, but before we tell you anything about it, you will have to sign this form.' He waved a piece of paper in the air, 'You will be signing the Official Secrets Act.'

We looked at each other uncertainly, not sure how to react.

'This means you cannot – *under any circumstances* – tell anyone what you will learn here, nor discuss the work you will be doing. This will cover you until thirty years after the end of the war.' He looked seriously at each of us. 'Anyone who refuses to sign will leave this room instantly and will be directed to other duties. Any questions?'

Nobody said a word. One by one, we all signed the official form. It would be long after the thirty years that I ever discussed the work I did with anybody.

My husband never knew, my son never knew.

Returning to our hut, we discussed what it could be that was so secret. 'Do you think we're going to be spies?' someone asked.

'Course not, we're only airwomen!'

I fell asleep with difficulty that night, wondering what to expect the next day and waiting for the 0600 hours wake-up call.

Our training would last three weeks. We were separated into three groups, each with a different job: Radar Operators, Operations Room Plotters and Filter Room

Plotters. Everybody had different skills, but there was one thing that we all had in common: we all had to speak 'the King's English' as it was then known, meaning that we could not have an accent of any sort. We had to make calculations as fast as possible and pass on information clearly and quickly. Our information had to be understood instantly – a thick accent might mean having to repeat yourself, and that could be the difference between life and death.

As we stood waiting for our names to be called, the WAAF Flight Officer looked at me and said just two words: 'Filter Plotter'.

The first two days were spent in lessons, learning how the Radar system worked and how it was used to help British fighter pilots, give air raid warnings, help rescue operations and instruct army gun crews for firing.

Everybody working in Radar Stations, Filter Rooms, and Operations Rooms were part of the 'Dowding System', named after Air Chief Marshal Sir Hugh

The Filter Room was central to Britain's Defence

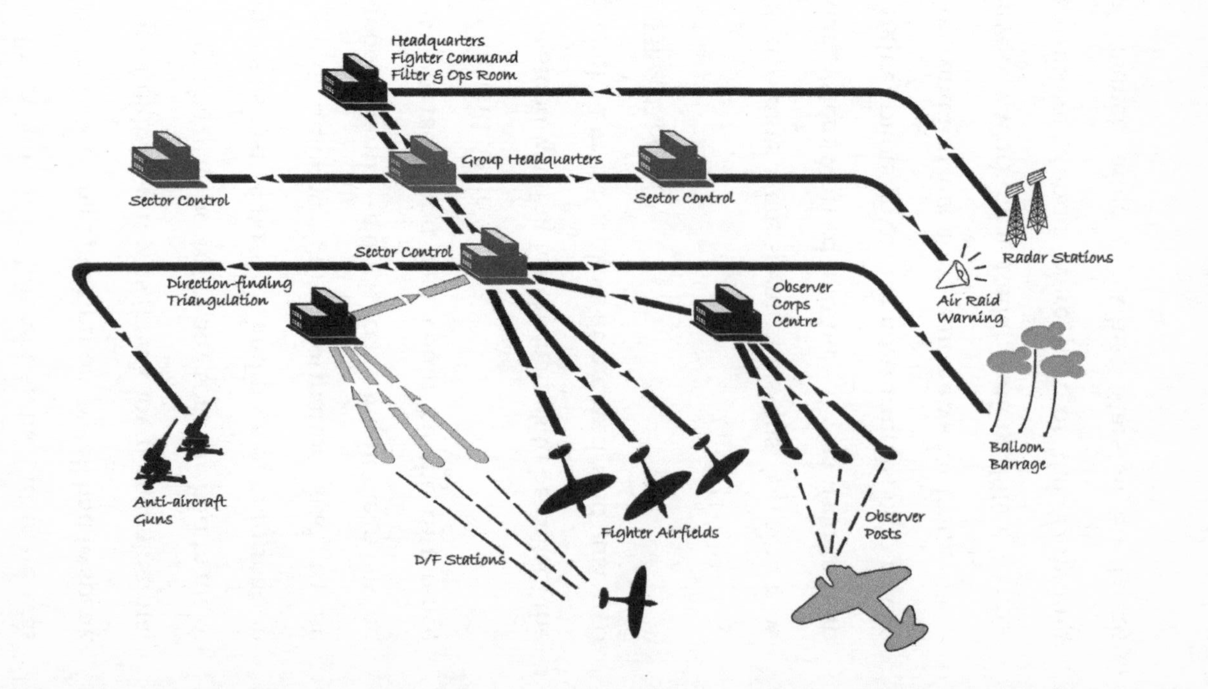

Dowding. This was like a wall of defence against enemy attacks, with different stages including new technology, ground defence and fighter aircraft.

The first line of defence was the Radar Stations. There was a chain of stations along the coast called Chain Home, overlapping each other so that no area was left unprotected. They sent out radio beams, which bounced off aircraft flying through British airspace.

The Radar Operators phoned their information through to the Filter Room.

Neighbouring Radar Stations saw a different signal from oncoming aircraft. One might have a good idea of their distance and height, while the next had a better

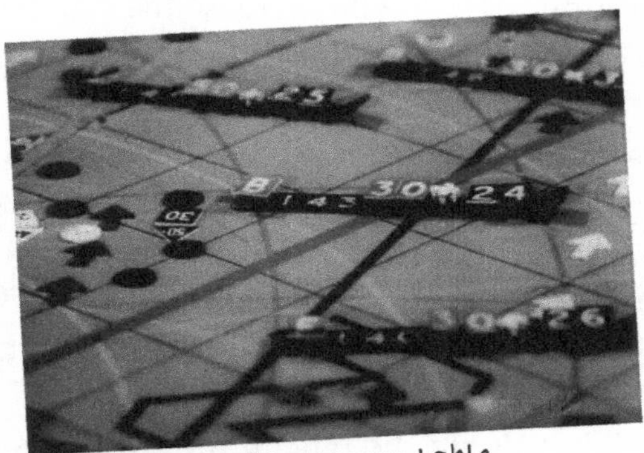

Filter Room table

indication of how many planes were coming.

The job of the Filter Room was to turn all this information into a complete picture.

Filter Plotters like me plotted the information on a big map table, using racks of different coloured counters showing the height, direction and number of aircraft.

On the balcony above, Tellers watched closely as the information was constantly updated and would decide if the aircraft were 'friendlies' or 'hostile.' Speed was essential, to tell our aircraft where they had to go to intercept an enemy raid.

Only the British aircraft could broadcast an IFF (Identification Friend or Foe) signal which identified them as friendly. They could increase the signal to act as an SOS if they were in trouble. We would give special attention to their location, and send Air Sea Rescue if they crashed into the sea.

Britain's air defence was divided into four Groups, and each had their own Filter Room. Winston Churchill called the Filter Room the lynchpin of Britain's defence

– the thing keeping it all together. This is where I would spend most of the war years.

If the incoming aircraft were identified as enemy planes by the Teller at the Filter Room, the information was passed on to the Group's Operations Rooms. Women working at the Operations Rooms were in contact with the Fighter Stations, and their job was to tell the controllers when they received the position of enemy aircraft. Plotters, sat around another table map, would move blocks and counters across the map as the raid progressed. A controller would view the information, and would decide where and when to send the squadrons

Filter Room, Fighter Command HQ

to take off and intercept – '*scramble*'.

Once the fighter squadrons were sent out, the controllers guided the pilots to intercept. Once the pilots could see the enemy planes, they radioed: 'Tally Ho!'

The information would also go to the gun crews so they could point their guns in the right direction, warn the country of possible air raids – and chains of enormous barrage balloons would be raised high in the sky to divert the enemy.

We didn't understand everything on the first day but already knew that we would be taking part in something vital to the defence of our country, and I think we all felt proud. I just hoped that I would be good enough to do my job properly.

On the second day we watched films of Radar Stations with their four enormous steel pylons, and lots of transmitting aerials. We saw the Radar operators sitting in front of their screens, with a pulsing light when a response was received. We saw the Operations Room with its large table map and the girls around it wearing headsets and moving the counters and markers with a long pole. It all seemed quite peaceful and organised.

The Filter Room was the complete opposite. It was buzzing with activity; girls crowded around the table putting down and taking away counters, officers having to push their way through them to put down their arrows, people shouting instructions down from the balconies.

We were told where we were being sent in our three groups – the ten Filter Plotters would be trained in one of the less busy Filter Rooms.

The next morning we walked into the training Filter Room. It was a large room, almost completely taken over by a strangely shaped table. Looking more closely, I could see that it followed the shape of the coastline from the north of Norfolk to the Isle of Wight. I realised that the whole table was in the shape of Britain, the English Channel, and even Holland, Belgium and France, all divided into large squares, each with two capital letters; AA, AB, AC, all the way through the alphabet. We took our places at the table, each seat in front of a headset.

We had to learn a different alphabet – Apple, Beer, Charlie, Dog and so on. Later on the Americans introduced the new code names (called the phonetic alphabet) for letters that are used today – Alpha, Bravo, Charlie, Delta – but I was trained never to forget the RAF codes. We were given a box of counters, coloured to match our station. My station was connected to Rye on the south coast, so my counters were green. I noticed that the counters had different shapes on them, and our next lesson was to learn the symbols. Circles meant the position, triangles meant the estimated number of aircraft and squares meant the estimated height. There were rectangular counters too; some marked with IFF, and some marked BIF (that was a Mayday code to give warning that an aircraft was in trouble).

We were given a test run, and plugged our headsets in. For a while we were just told to listen. A man's voice announced: 'New track, Victor Willie 9-1, 4-3, 15 plus at 20, showing IFF.'

At first none of this made any sense to me, but after practicing for a while I was able to understand the instructions.

'Right,' said the squadron leader. 'That's enough for this morning. Go for your lunch.'

As we ate our lunch in the Mess hall, everyone admitted it was hard to take it all in. Joan White, the girl who had sat next to me in the Filter Room, looked worried and said, 'I'm sure I'll never be able to do this!'

I did my best to encourage her, 'We're all finding it difficult, it'll be fine.'

As the afternoon went on I was getting quicker and quicker at putting down the right counters. The table was now covered with coloured counters and things began to take shape. I was getting the hang of it – I felt like I was in battle myself!

CHAPTER FIFTEEN

Each day there was more to learn. There was only one girl who was not improving, and by the fifth day she was nowhere to be seen. She had been taken off Special Duties and sent back to RAF Innsworth.

On the last day we were given one final test before we were told where we would be sent. There were seven Filter Rooms in the whole of Britain and Northern Ireland, and we could be sent to any except Fighter Command Headquarters at Stanmore, where the most activity was. Squadron Leader Mann told us, 'You'll have to prove that you're fast and accurate before you get to Fighter Command.'

I was told I would be posted to 10 Group, the Filter Room based in Rudloe Manor, near Bath. The Filter Room would cover the coast from the Isle of Wight to the north of Wales. They told me there would be a lot of enemy action in this sector, bombing our ports and the many air bases in the area. My poor cousin Eric's parents, my auntie and uncle, lived near Bath, so I was excited to hear that I would be near to family. I couldn't wait to get there.

My journey to my new posting took me through Paddington and then on another train to Bath. Once again, passing through London, I saw houses with their roofs torn off with whole walls missing, like dolls houses.

Life at Rudloe Manor was different to my experiences at Innsworth and Leighton Buzzard. When I first arrived, I was shocked when I was taken underground!

There were vast caves under the camp, stretching in all directions. Even today, under the rolling Wiltshire countryside are mile upon mile of tunnels, a maze of long forgotten military sites.

I was in C Watch, and never worked the same hours. The days were split into three different watches, from 0800 to 1600 hours, 1600 hours to midnight, and then midnight to 0800 hours. We stayed in local civilian houses called billets, and I would be picked up from my billet an hour before my watch started, to get a meal at the base. If I went off-camp I had to report back in time for duty – 'No exceptions,' warned the sergeant.

Rudloe Manor

Work in the Filter Room continued over twenty-four hours. Hitler's Luftwaffe did not stop at night, so neither did we. If it wasn't a busy watch we might get a quarter of an hour break, so we could go for a cup of coffee and a sandwich. If there was a lot of air activity, of course we could not leave our posts. We worked underground to protect us from being bombed. In those days the air conditioning and heating systems were not very efficient so it was not an easy or comfortable job.

Some days we would be busy every moment we were on duty; if the weather was bad, no aircraft could fly and the hours crawled by like years. But we were all proud to think we were helping to defend our country.

Most of C Watch was staying in billets in Corsham. At one o'clock in the morning after my first shift, we were brought up to the surface from the Filter Room in a lift and then sent straight to the Mess for supper. The house where I was staying was almost the last on the journey as we were dropped off one by one. I crept upstairs and fell into bed, exhausted.

It was my first day and I had plotted some Nazi bombers that were aiming to attack the docks at Plymouth!

In the morning, I found that I was in a large detached

house with a lovely garden looking out over fields. Another girl, Ruth Hibberd, and I were staying in the house owned by Mr and Mrs Clarke, who owned the local coal merchants. They told me I could use the kitchen during the day when they weren't there and make my own meals, but I had to bring my own food from the camp as their rations were only small.

Because I could use my right and left hands equally, during every session in the Filter Rooms I was becoming faster and more confident, and after three months I was told I was going to be promoted.

It was August and the weather was sticky and hot. After a busy night watch, Ruth and I decided to sleep on the grass in the garden in our pyjamas. Around midday, I was woken up by Mrs Clarke who had come home for lunch.

'You're wanted on the phone. They said it's urgent.'

My stomach lurched. What had I done wrong? There was a message to report immediately to Wing Commander Rudd's office. I had recently applied for a

position to be an Intelligence Officer, and so I wondered if it could be a response. I dressed quickly and was picked up by transport and arrived at the Wingco's office in record time.

'Sit down,' he said. 'I have called you in to tell you I am putting you forward for a commission as a Filterer Officer. I think you will do well.'

I was confused. 'But, sir, I have just applied to an Intelligence Commission.'

'You won't get it. I'll make sure of that. We need good Filterers desperately and that's what you will be.' He was very firm. 'You can go now.'

Returning to Corsham I was thinking very hard. What did I want to do? Would I have any choice?

A week later, I was invited to be interviewed for an Intelligence Commission, and two days later I reported to Air Ministry. The officer at reception told me to go to Room 153 and wait. I went up to the first floor and found the room. I knocked, but there was no reply. I knocked again, still nothing, so I opened the door. The room was empty. I sat down at the desk and waited. High up on the far wall were three small windows looking down into the room. Several people appeared and gazed down at me and then moved on. I don't know exactly how long I waited, but it was well over an hour and a half and still nobody appeared. Finally, I got up and left with the wing commander's promise a few days earlier in my ears: 'There's no point in you going, you know. I'll stop it.'

Instead, I was put forward to become a Filterer

Officer, just as the wing commander had said. This meant I would be a higher rank and not an ordinary airwoman, and all the airmen and airwomen would have to salute me.

Another new challenge.

CHAPTER SIXTEEN

I was sent on a three week training course to Bawdsey Manor in Suffolk. In 1937, a scientist named Robert Watson Watt, together with his team, had come to Bawdsey Manor when they invented Radar.

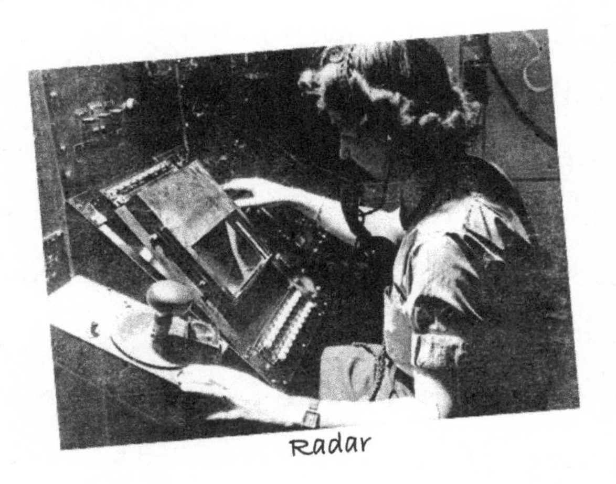

Radar

The RAF base was in a large Victorian manor house with tall towers and beautiful steps leading up to the entrance, set on a cliff overlooking the North Sea. We had to travel to the nearest railway station at Felixstowe and then take a ferry the rest of the way. The beaches below were all surrounded by barbed wire fencing and were mined to prevent the Germans from attempting to land there, so there was no chance of swimming.

It was a very concentrated course and it wasn't easy. The work was demanding and the hours were long. One of the other girls on the course, called Sylvia, a plotter from 13 Group, found it especially difficult. On just the second day of practice everybody had become a lot quicker at understanding the information plotted on the table, except for Sylvia. She became more and more upset until she cried, 'I can't go on!' and burst into tears. She ran out of the room, and by the time we returned to the Manor she was packing her bags.

On the final day, we were given a written test and one last filtering session while we waited for the results. All five of us who were left had passed. We were all given our white officer cadet bands to wear around our hats, and sent to the Officers Cadet Training Unit in

Loughborough College, where we would have to pass an officers' course. If we passed, we would go on to a Filter Room.

'Cadet Officer le Croissette, you will be reporting to 9 Group, RAF Barton Hall, Preston. Good luck.'

There were five of us who arrived in Loughborough that August, 1941, for just one week of training. My head felt filled to the brim with RAF language – AWOL, absent without leave; DRO, daily routine orders. My legs ached from marching and my right arm from saluting. On the final day we were all told that we had passed, and would go on to the Filter Rooms. I was given a new title – Assistant Section Officer – and fifty pounds to get a special uniform made by a tailor.

New Filterer Officers were always sent to a quieter area to begin with until they became faster. The station in Preston covered the coast defence from the north of Wales up to Scotland.

After a short weekend at home with my mother and

father, I set off to my next adventure with my new airwoman's uniform, kitbag, suitcase and gas mask. As I walked down the street to the bus stop, an airman passed me, turned his head towards me and saluted. I was so surprised I almost forgot to salute back!

Something else I've got to get used to, I thought.

After spending time in the busy Filter Room in Bath, 9 Group was quite dull. There wasn't much to do in our spare time, and the local people were quite unfriendly! There wasn't much enemy activity, so the nights were often long and boring and the bunkers were very cold. Lots of the workers took books with them, or did sewing or knitting to keep themselves occupied on the night watches.

One day, during a particularly slow shift, an approaching aircraft caught my attention. The flight was coming from Ireland, but didn't match with any known movements, and it wasn't showing IFF identification. I tracked the path closely, trying to tell if the plane was a German bomber. About fifty miles from the coast, it was finally recognised as Winston Churchill! The prime minister was returning from a meeting with the American President Roosevelt, and the plane's pilot had forgotten to turn on his IFF signal. Thank goodness I didn't send any fighter planes to attack!

After six months at Barton Hall, I was excited (and relieved!) to hear that I was ready to become a section officer, the equivalent of a first lieutenant in the Army. Even better news, I was being posted back to 10 Group, Rudloe Manor. It was like going home.

Returning to Rudloe Manor as a section officer instead of a new recruit was very different. I had a lovely room to myself on the main camp instead of lodging with local couples, and I even had a maid, or 'batwoman' – no more bed-making for me! There was a much friendlier atmosphere; I already knew lots of the WAAF and RAF officers from my time as a plotter.

It was far more interesting than 9 Group at Preston. There was a lot more activity, and there was a lot more going on when I was off-duty too. We often had fighter pilots sent to the base for a break after they had completed a tour. Most of them were daredevils, always up to something. They would challenge anybody who was brave enough to take a running jump from about twenty yards away and dive through the hatch in the Mess hall. Those who failed, despite the knocks and bruises, still had to buy drinks all round.

One day the pilots decided to fold my friend and fellow Section Officer Jane Asherson in half and put her in a large waste paper basket. She fitted perfectly!

Not everybody I met was quite so much fun. Working at 10 Group, I met a man named Rex Harrison, a captain in the Signals Corps who served as an Air Raid Warnings Officer in the Operations Room. Rex made little effort to mix with the rest of us, but he made sure we knew how important he was. I particularly disliked him because of his table manners. He would stuff his mouth with toast and marmalade and eat so messily that the soggy bread would ooze out of the side of his mouth. Disgusting! He would later become a very famous film star.

The months went on. That Christmas, our watch thought it was a good idea to put on the pantomime, *Aladdin*. We knew it was important to have some light-hearted fun to help with the demanding days and nights of the work in the Filter Room.

In February, a new air chief marshal, Arthur Harris, took control of Bomber Command, and started planning new strategies. He decided that targeting a smaller city with military bases in Germany would be more successful than targeting a bigger industrial city. He chose a city called Lubeck.

The British bombers planned to hit on the night of March 28th, 1942. Lubeck had a port and a submarine base nearby, but even more importantly it was mostly built from wood. The reports came back that the city went up in flames, and the raid was a success.

Hitler was furious and ordered a series of raids against historic British towns. These were named the Baedeker Raids. As a well-known Nazi campaigner, Baron Gustav von Sturm, famously promised: 'We shall go out and bomb every building marked with three stars in the Baedeker Tourist Guide.' On the evening of April 23rd, they began.

In the 10 Group Filter Room we plotted and tracked lots of enemy aircraft crossing the south coast of Britain. Exeter was first, and was bombed two nights in a row; on the night of the 25th it was Bath's turn. I was on duty from 1600 hours until midnight. For the first two hours, the table was empty – no activity. We all thought we were in for a quiet watch. We sat and waited, some of us read books while others chatted amongst themselves and to their Radar operators on the telephone. And then everything changed. Suddenly, around eighty hostile aircraft were reported crossing the south coast from France.

Deep underground in the Filter Room we couldn't hear anything, but people in the main camp above ground heard the bombers overhead. We were only about eight miles away. Only after our watch was finished, and we came up into the fresh air, did we see the fires glowing as the city burned. I was suddenly terrified for my aunt and uncle. I rushed to the phones early the following morning, but all the lines were down, and that night the Germans returned. The next morning, I was finally allowed to leave the camp to find out what had happened.

Luckily, my family was safe. I was so relieved to see my aunt open the front door, and although there was a hole in the roof and no glass in the windows, the damage to their house wasn't quite as bad as I imagined. She told me that they had rushed to their shelter when they heard the sirens, and had been terrified when they heard the bombs sounding so close. On the first night, when it all went quiet, they returned to the house.

The second night was worse. A bomb dropped very near, and they could even feel the vibration in the shelter. In the morning, they came up to see how much damage had been done. An incendiary, the bombs which started fires, had dropped through their roof. Luckily it was a dud and had just fizzled out without causing too much harm. They both looked very pale, but seemed to be coping. 'There are many much worse off than us,' my aunt insisted.

The damage to that beautiful city was appalling. There were four hundred casualties. It was only when I arrived back at camp that I learned that three of our Plotters had been in Bath with their husbands or boyfriends for a short break. The hotel where they were staying had suffered a direct hit, and they had all been killed. The following night, everybody was shaken and we all found it hard to concentrate.

The airwomen working in the Filter Rooms were usually between the ages of nineteen and twenty-three years old. We had to become adults as early as sixteen and meet the wartime challenges. Try to imagine how these girls felt as they plotted the enemy attacking their homes. Some of them had brothers, husbands or boyfriends in the Air Force, Navy or Army. Some days we might track five hundred of our bombers on a raid; four hundred might return safely, but the rest might have gone off course and been damaged, and some would never make it, crashing into the Channel as they tried to reach home. The girls would always wonder if their loved ones had been killed or injured during any of the enemy raids, if they were the ones that failed to come home. This is why we were so proud of them. They never let us down, nobody fainted, nobody cried out, and nobody failed to turn up on duty. They were marvellous. All this time, we never told anyone what we did, not even our parents. Remember that we had signed the Official

Secrets Act. Many of the people I worked with have told me their families never knew the important work the Filter Room did in those wartime days.

Some months later I was called into Wing Commander Rudd's office. By this time, I had been put in charge of A Watch, which meant a lot more responsibility.

'Eileen, you've done well here. We've been asked to send replacement Filterer Officer to Fighter Command HQ. I'm recommending you. How do you feel about that?'

'Delighted,' I replied, 'although I have loved working here.'

'Right, take a week's leave and then report to Stanmore.'

It was early June 1943, and I was being sent to the busiest Filter Room; 11 Group, Fighter Command Headquarters. I remembered Squadron Leader Mann's words from years before. 'You'll have to prove that you're fast enough before you get to Fighter Command, but I'm sure some of you will get there one day.'

CHAPTER SEVENTEEN

I had written a letter to George, giving him my new address, the day after I arrived at Stanmore. The few letters I received from him were now arriving in the form of airgraphs. These were introduced because otherwise heavy cargoes of letters would have to be brought back to Britain by sea, from our troops serving overseas, which was a risk for the Navy. All letters were now photographed and airlifted home, so we received them more quickly. I had received an airgraph telling me he was serving overseas but little else; his letters mostly said he was well but missing me.

Then several weeks passed and I had heard no more but I was used to this. However when Christmas came and I still had no news of George, and getting no replies to my letters, I began to worry.

One day in early January 1944, I received a letter in a handwriting I didn't recognise, with a British stamp. It was from George's younger sister, Mary. I thought at first she was writing to tell me he had been killed, but no – she was breaking the news to me that George had married a girl in Cairo. I was stunned.

After the initial shock, I began to understand. After all, we had seen little of each other in the last three years. I wrote back to Mary and said I understood and to tell George I wished him luck. I was heartbroken, but my mother was almost more upset than I was. She was very fond of George and already saw him as a son-in-law. It wasn't until many years later when George got in touch with me that he told me she had written him a very angry letter.

I quickly settled in to my new life at Fighter Command, and was soon a firmly established member of No. 2 Officers' mess. We had some great laughs!

One night during the winter months, the thatched

roof of the Officers' Mess hall caught fire. We always had a roaring log fire, and one afternoon the beam must have become so heated that it caused the thatch to ignite. A friend of mine, Mary Hogg, and I climbed on to the roof with fire extinguishers. They were quite difficult to turn on. Mary eventually started hers, but accidentally pointed it in my direction. The back of my uniform jacket and skirt were soaked!

There was no time to change, so having put out the fire, we went straight on duty. About half an hour later, to my horror my skirt disintegrated thanks to the acid in the extinguishers and almost dropped off! To save my modesty, I was rushed back to the billet to put on a replacement uniform. Luckily, the insurance company paid for a new skirt.

One joke we created in Fighter Command was about Lottie Crump, a newly arrived section officer who was attached to B Watch. We told the male officers what a great girl she was – and very pretty. They were all anxious to meet her, but they never did. She never seemed to turn up for watch duties, though her footprint appeared on the ceiling of the anteroom, duly signed to join all the rest.

The fact was she never existed. We had invented her, and we kept up the game for over two months. We always had excuses for her non-appearance – she would be off on a special course, she was in sick bay, the head admin officer wanted to see her! Finally, we posted Lottie off to another Filter Room.

Occasionally, Filterer Officers were instructed to go to

Bawdsey Manor to train new male Filterers, and on one such time I was sent. While I was there we were told that all the women had to take lessons in shooting. We were all dressed in battledress and, with our short hair, we were likely to become targets should the Germans land on the beaches. We were all given Sten guns that you had to shoot from the hip instead of rifles, and practiced for several days. We stood on the side of cliff shooting out to sea, but it was difficult to see how accurate we were.

By the end, our hips were extremely bruised from the impact of the weapon as we shot, but we felt like we could protect ourselves. One thing that amused me about this rather serious training – we received complaints from the fishermen in the bay who said they were being peppered with our shots even though they were far out to sea!

Prime Minister Winston Churchill often came to Fighter Command Headquarters to discuss plans with the air chief marshal. If he learned there was an expected big

German bombing raid, he would come into the Filter Room and look over the balcony, watching events as they happened. Churchill famously loved cigars and always had one stuck in his mouth, but when he visited the Filter Room he never lit them. I think it was a comfort to him, with all the terrible things going on and the hard decisions he had to make.

As the war went on, the government needed more advanced aircraft, and developments in technology cost money. They launched a national savings programme called *Wings for Victory,* encouraging the public to buy savings stamps and certificates to provide extra funds.

Fighter Command HQ issued a notice asking all watches to organise a public event to advertise the programme. A prize of £200 savings certificates would be awarded to the watch raising the most savings from the public. B Watch had a meeting and decided to run a garden party in the grounds of Hill House, and I was asked to head the campaign, with a committee of five people. We contacted local shopkeepers and companies and had a great response with offers of many items as prizes for the raffle. I had noticed a riding school opposite the house, with small ponies as well as larger horses. I decided to call and ask if the owner would lend two ponies and perhaps a stable-girl to offer rides for the children. I didn't realise what a difference to my life that visit would make.

I knocked on the door and a middle-aged man answered, who I guessed was the owner. He was dressed in breeches and riding boots, and had a weathered complexion. 'Can I help you?' he asked. I explained we were trying to raise funds for the Wings for Victory campaign. He immediately invited me in. He introduced himself as Captain Jimmy Younghusband, and offered to provide two children's ponies and advertise the event to his clients. Sure enough, on the day the two ponies arrived. The weather was kind, the sun shone and the public poured in. At the end of a busy afternoon, we presented the many raffle prizes and thanked the public for their support. Later, we were told that we had won the £200 saving certificates.

A few days after the party, I went over to the riding school to thank Captain Younghusband for his help and let him know how well we had done. I was invited in for a cup of tea and met his son Peter, who was on leave from nearby RAF Northolt. He was also the drummer in the RAF station dance band. We chatted for a while and he suggested I should book the band for the next dance we would run in the Mess. His father also mentioned that there were two large ponds in his grounds, and if any of us from the Mess wanted to use them to swim we only had to ask. A week later several of us took up the offer.

It was a warm June day after a tiring night watch and we made our way across the field near Stanmore Common. We wore our bathing suits under our uniform, so we could strip off and dive in. The water was ice cold but so refreshing! Back on dry land we soon fell asleep on the grass. About half an hour later we heard someone say, 'Hello, there. Enjoy your swim?' It was Peter, home for a few hours.

And that's how it all began.

Over the next weeks we spent any free time we had together. I took him over to meet my parents and on one occasion he took my grandfather to the local pub. On my birthday some weeks later Peter asked me to marry him, and on September 30th that year we were married.

My wedding

When I returned to the RAF camp newly engaged with my ring, my friend Kat Turner said, 'I didn't think it would be long. You've been spending so much time at the Spring Ponds; I couldn't imagine you went there only for the swimming!'

CHAPTER EIGHTEEN

On June 6th 1944 I came on duty with B Watch at midnight and knew immediately that something important was happening.

The strength of Radar technology had been constantly improving, and it could now reach down as far as sea level. That night on the Filter Room table there were many plots displayed in the Channel registering a height of zero feet – that meant ships. It could only mean one thing; a possible landing by our troops once more on European soil. These were the vessels taking our soldiers and armaments to be landed on the beaches of Normandy.

It was D-Day, code named Operation Neptune; the day that Britain would return to France with our allies, the Americans and the Polish, and fight back. As the night progressed, more and more landings were made.

The Germans were caught unaware.

In order to keep our landing sites secret, we gave the enemy false information that Pas de Calais, on the Normandy coast, would be the target area. Fake military tanks, machine guns and other vehicles were made of cardboard and positioned on the fields of southern England, where they expected us to make our departure to the Normandy coast. German aircraft had spied these and reported them, and the German Army chiefs had massed forces on the coast there ready to defend against the landings. The plan had worked. The D-Day landings took them by surprise and the Allies managed to get a strong foothold within a short space of time.

Triggered by the successful landing of the Allied Forces in Nazi-occupied France, the Germans took revenge and launched their secret weapon against London four days later – the V1 flying bomb. It was the first aircraft that flew without a pilot, named after the German word for vengeance, *vergeitung.* This weapon had a terrifying effect. Launched from underground tunnels from the coast of France, it would fly on a straight course. When it ran out of fuel, it would fall to the ground and explode. We used to call them buzz bombs because of the noise, or 'Doodlebugs'. This was typical of the Londoners' sense of humour even in the midst of danger.

The people of London soon learned to recognise the buzzing sound of the V1 engine, and when it cut out they would run for their lives to the nearest shelter.

Our fighter pilots quickly learned how to tip the wings of the Doodlebugs causing it to drop to the ground.

They always chose a safe area to attack the bombs, away from the city, so they often landed in fields in Kent or exploded in mid-air. Our guns on the coast would target the bombs as they approached to try and stop them from reaching their targets. But the V1 caused many deaths in London.

The distance the V1s could fly depended on how much fuel they had in their tanks, so false landing information was sent out and the Germans were tricked into thinking they were landing north of their intended target, London. To correct this, they put less fuel in the tanks and the V1s then landed in the open country areas of Kent, causing far less damage. There were many people who worked secretly on this sort of counter intelligence. Even now we don't know all the incredible things they managed to do.

Another memorable watch when history was made was the night of June 16th. An engineer called Barnes Wallis had invented a special bomb for this raid, called Operation Chastise. It could be dropped on to a water surface and directed towards the target; it would bounce across the water like skimming a stone. Bomber Command was targeting a series of dams in Germany – the Mohne, the Eder and the Sorpe. The mission was to destroy the dams and flood the Ruhr valley where many of the Germany factories were sited. They hoped that the damage would take up to two years to repair, and the supplies and replacements to the enemy would be halted.

Operation Chastise was completed by the famous 617 Squadron, put together especially for this mission and made up of 113 men in nineteen planes. They were led by Wing Commander Guy Gibson, who later won a Victoria Cross for leading this raid.

That night, I was on watch in the Filter Room. As I started tracking the first outgoing bombers, I realised that this was something quite different from any other raid we had undertaken. Normally, all the aircraft would join up together over the English Channel and then go out in a mass raid, but this time they went in three waves. Nine aircraft were in the first group. It was fifteen minutes later when the next five aircraft followed on a slightly different route, to confuse the Germans. Then the third group went off, again a quarter of an hour later, following the first wave's route.

Gibson, leading the first group, made ten runs across the Mohne dam, searching for the best angle to drop the bomb. He had to fly very low and with his spotlights on; a very risky tactic, as it left his aircraft open to attack. Fortunately this didn't happen, but when the bomb was dropped it only broke part of the dam.

The second aircraft was then diverted back to have another go and eventually managed to destroy the Mohne dam. The following bombers destroyed the Eder dam as well, but the Sorpe was only slightly damaged. Even so, the bombs caused vast flooding in the Ruhr and Eder valleys.

The Germans managed to repair the damage done to the factories in about six months, a much shorter period than expected. It was estimated that 1,600 people drowned in the Ruhr valley, and sadly many of these were either prisoners of war or factory workers from the countries Germany had invaded.

Of the nineteen British aircraft sent as Dam Busters, eight were damaged or shot down, and fifty-three airmen were killed, and three were captured. Perhaps it wasn't the success that Bomber Command had hoped, but nobody could deny the bravery shown by the Dam Buster crews and, of course, the unique contribution made by Doctor Barnes Wallis with his amazing bouncing bomb. Even if the raid didn't have the long-term effect originally expected, it had an enormous impact on the British people. We were all behind them.

CHAPTER NINETEEN

Meanwhile we had found out that Hitler had another secret weapon, the V2 rocket, and it was supersonic, which meant it could fly faster than the speed of sound. The RAF 'Photo Freddies', aircraft that flew fast and high with special cameras but no guns, had taken pictures of something suspicious at Peenemunde off the Baltic Coast in Germany. A WAAF photographic interpreter at the Royal Air Force Photographic Unit at Benson recognised from the burned ground that a supersonic rocket could have been launched there. But how would we deal with this in the Filter Room? When was it coming, and where would it land?

The code name adopted for this new threat was Operation Big Ben. We were told that if any plotter received a message from their Radar Station saying Big

Ben, the nearest Filterer had to shout out the warning.

It was September 8th when the first V2 rocket was launched against Britain. I was on duty that night. 'Not much doing so far!' another officer told me as we swapped. I took my place at the table and filtered a few Coastal Command patrols and a fighter exercise off Tangmere. I took a short break at 0430 hours; it was still fairly quiet. At 0745 hours a plotter jumped out of her seat, obviously excited. 'Ma'am, my operator has just said "Big Ben"!'

I realised that this was the warning, and it was up

to me to give the signal. I jumped up on a chair and shouted: 'Big Ben, Big Ben, Big Ben!' (We had to shout it three times.) The effect was immediate.

The Controller pressed a warning bell, telling everybody on his list that we had received this signal. The balcony sprang to life, people leaning over the balcony to watch the table below, phones ringing. I had no idea at the time that I had announced the first V2 rocket to be launched against London.

It was a day to be remembered.

Five rockets had been launched from the base at Pas de Calais; two had crashed as soon as they were launched, one was launched at Paris, and two were launched at London. One V2 had landed at Chiswick in the London suburbs; there was no warning, no siren. It was something new. Three people were killed and seventeen injured. The houses that were destroyed made the area look like a battlefield. Can you imagine the fear that this new weapon inflicted on the people of London? Because it was supersonic it landed before it could be heard. That was bad enough, but as the days passed, more and more V1 and V2 bombs fell on London and Kent, and then there were rumours of a third V weapon – the population wondered what terror they would face next.

These raids were so different from the bombing of the Blitz when people could see and hear the aircraft and knew that our fighters were up there fighting back.

CHAPTER TWENTY

By now our troops in France, together with the Americans, were having some success. After fierce battles, they managed to force the Germans to retreat and had taken the Pas de Calais launch sites of the V2s. Eight thousand German soldiers escaped when the Allied Forces liberated Pas de Calais. The German's managed to move their equipment north to Rotterdam.

V2

In the meantime, we had developed a Radar device which could track the curved path of the V2 rockets.

The V2 could only travel so far, just about three hundred miles, and from their new launch base in

Rotterdam they could no longer reach London, so the target was changed to Antwerp. Britain had captured the port at Antwerp before the Germans could destroy it. The ports at Calais and Boulogne had been damaged so much before the Germans left that we could not use them. Antwerp was the first available port where troops and supplies could land, and was a very important target for the enemy.

British engineers had developed Mobile Radar Units which were able to track the curve of the rockets so we could trace them back to their launch sites, and these were sent to Europe. On November 19th, 106 MARU (Mobile Advance Reporting Unit) was put together. Eight Filterer Officers were chosen to deal with this new challenge. I was told I would be sent overseas.

I had only been married for three months when I was ordered to go to 33 Wing, part of the 2nd Tactical Air Force (TAF). I would be going to Belgium!

I wasn't able to tell my husband why I was going. He couldn't understand why I was being sent abroad. Since our honeymoon we had only met five times and once again we were to be separated, not knowing when I was likely to return.

'Why you?' he demanded when I broke the news. He was desperately upset and couldn't understand why I couldn't tell him what I was going to do. I had forgotten to tell him that I had signed the Official Secrets Act. Despite this, I realised it was important work we were going to do. We had to stop the V2s being aimed at our only usable port.

We were sent to a town called Malines, midway between Antwerp and the capital of Belgium, Brussels. The Nazis were now launching the rockets from trailers drawn by trucks. They would leave their base and hide in the woods, on a beach or even in a car park in a nearby town. They would launch the rocket and then prepare to return to base. But first it was essential to unload all the high octane fuel that remained before they could leave the site. It would be twenty minutes before they were able to drive off. This was the total time we had to find the target and destroy it.

I arrived in Malines in early December 1944 and, as there was no room to stay in the Officers' Mess, I was to be placed in the home of a local Flemish family, an artist named Ignace Kennis and his wife. I didn't know at the time, but in Belgium some residents spoke Flemish and some spoke French, and there was no love lost between the two. When I arrived, I spoke to the couple in French and I guess they were not too happy about that. They were not at all friendly and told me I had to keep to my room and if I wanted to eat anything, I would have to provide it. Belgium, like Holland, was very short of food supplies so I suppose it was understandable. I was also told that as fuel for heating was rationed, I could only have two baths a week. Monsieur Kennis was a tall, gloomy looking man; his wife, small and timid. They both looked pale and under fed.

They weren't very young, and possibly they weren't too happy to have me staying with them, although they

must have received some payment for their trouble. I couldn't see myself spending much time in this house.

To reach it, I had to walk across the town; very creepy after coming off duty at midnight, especially when I had to go through the covered Butter Market. It was an ancient stone structure with a slate roof and cobbled floor. The first time I walked through, the sound of my heels echoed around the building, so I tried to make as little noise as possible in future. I would always wonder if someone was hiding there. Although there was a night time ban on the public going out in the area, we never knew whether the Germans had left any of their troops behind to act as spies. This was one of the only times I felt really frightened – it was the unknown. I often wished I had a companion, and wondered what Peter was doing.

We worked round the clock, again in eight-hour watches, sometimes tracking many V2s, sometimes none. All the time the position of the launch sites was changing as our troops were gaining more ground and forcing the German army to retreat. Always the target was Antwerp and the docks. Three hundred more V2s landed there than on London, killing hundreds of citizens. This went on for four months, every day and every night. If the weather was bad our Mosquito bombers could not take off, so there were more V2s landing successfully on the port those days. Slowly we destroyed more and more of their launch lorries.

Our job was to calculate where the Germans were

launching the rockets from each time. It took two minutes to receive the position on the curve of the rocket from the mobile Radar units. Using a slide rule, which looked like a normal ruler but was used for calculations, we used this position combined with the position of where the rocket had fallen, which we called 'fall of shot'. Then we could trace back the launch curve to where it had begun its flight from the truck. This all had to be completed in five minutes.

This position was sent to the Intelligence section, who notified the nearest aircraft in that area. We always had several sections of Mosquito bombers patrolling day and night. When the pilots received the location of the launch trucks, they could target them. This technique was so successful that we managed to destroy all the vehicles by March 1945. Because our bombing raids had destroyed many of the German factories, it meant they were unable to replace the launch vehicles although they had masses of V2 rockets.

Despite duty hours, which were very concentrated,

and living conditions that were fairly bleak, we managed to have a good time when off duty as well as feeling we were doing something worthwhile.

Amongst the personnel of 33 Wing we found we had enough hockey players to form a team, a mixture of WAAF, RAF and Army. Nightclubs were reopening in Brussels and often a group of us would spend an evening there. More airwomen had joined us, taking over some of the kitchen and admin duties from the men who were being moved on.

We decided to make a club for them. We were given a ground floor flat that had been abandoned by the

Germans, and we did what we could to make a place to relax. We borrowed a few things to make the club more comfortable – chairs, a radio, and items to use in the kitchen.

Two weeks before Christmas I was told I was being sent back to Britain for three days to choose some extra items to make the conditions better for the WAAF. I managed to let Peter know and he met me as the plane landed. Peter told me that he had been so upset when I left, that he tried to smuggle himself into a plane going to Ghent. Of course he was found but, lucky for him, the pilot knew him and he was never reported.

I managed to pay a brief visit to my parents' home as well. I was horrified to find the house opposite had been destroyed by a V2. My mother hadn't told me, but our house had received considerable blast damage and she had been injured.

'Why didn't you tell me?' I asked.

'Well, I didn't want to worry you,' was her reply. I

felt terrible to think that I hadn't been there. It made me realise how much people had suffered, especially in London, but also how strong they were to not be beaten.

CHAPTER TWENTY-ONE

Christmas passed with little time for celebration. There had been heavy snowfall all over Belgium which stopped our aircraft from flying, and the Germans took advantage of this, increasing V2 launches against Antwerp day and night. The V2 rockets could fly in any weather.

Meanwhile in Russia, the Germans were losing more and more troops. Hitler decided on a new plan. It was at this time that the German army tried to split the American and British forces who were trying to join up together, to force them to make an agreement that benefited Germany. They launched an attack in the forest of the Ardennes, beginning the *Battle of the Bulge.* It lasted from December 16th until January 25th, when the German forces were defeated. What we did not realise was that Hitler's army were aiming to get to Antwerp, which would mean they had to capture Malines, so we could have become prisoners of war. Although we knew the battle was going on, we did not realise how lucky we were not to have been caught up in it.

On the 3rd February, my Belgian friend, Pierre asked me if I had a day off and, if so, would I like a day out. He owned a timber company and he had a mill in the Ardennes forest cutting the trees. He needed to collect more stock for his company, but also wanted to see whether the mill had been destroyed during the fighting there, and check that his workers were safe. So we set off early the next morning, driving through areas where there had obviously been a lot of fighting. There had been heavy snow storms and the snow was only just melting.

As we entered the forest, we could see German tanks, American tanks and British tanks, all mixed in with each other. Even more upsetting were the bodies of fallen soldiers, partially covered in the snow. I shuddered as we passed. We saw American uniforms, British uniforms and the grey uniforms of the enemy, Hitler's army. We were both horrified with what we were seeing. It was like a terrible dream. This was the first time I ever saw such a horrific sight.

The only good thing to happen that day was when we found that Pierre's mill was intact and all his workers safe. He was relieved but, like me, appalled at what must have been a fierce and bloody battle.

We moved on to the town of Bastogne, where a major battle had taken place. The Germans had tried to prevent the American forces, which were coming through France, from joining up with the British forces. Their goal was to reach the harbour at Antwerp and destroy it before the Allied Forces could rejoin. The Germans had to seize the roadways through eastern Belgium. Because all seven of the main roads in the Ardennes mountain range joined in Bastogne, it was vital that the Germans had control of the small town. The battle here lasted seven days, until additional forces managed to break through the Germans surrounding the American troops.

As we passed through, we could see that most of the buildings were destroyed. The few people we saw looked desperate as they trudged through the streets looking for food. We did not talk much as we were too upset with what we had seen that terrible day.

The launching of the V2s continued until the beginning of March 1945, but they were getting fewer and fewer as time went by. By mid March they had almost stopped. But we were still on duty each day as we had been warned that Intelligence had found out that a third Vengeance weapon was being prepared. What would this new terror be?

Meanwhile the Allied troops were forcing their way through the countries once occupied by Hitler's army, and were over the border into Germany itself. We were hoping that the end of the war was on the horizon.

CHAPTER TWENTY-TWO

At midday on May 8th peace in Europe had finally been declared. I came off duty at 0800. It had been a quiet night. As I crossed the road to go to the Officers' Mess for my breakfast, a little black Volkswagen car pulled up with a jerk in front of me.

RAF PILOTS

Two RAF pilots jumped out, hugged me and gave me a great big kiss! 'Aren't we glad to see you! You're the first

English girl we've seen since 1940!' said one of the pilots.

After recovering from the shock, I noticed that written on the front mudguard of this little German car were the letters *PWX!*

They explained that they were prisoners of war – now 'ex'! They were Wellington bomber pilots who had been shot down in 1940 and they had been in a prison camp ever since. Five days before they had noticed that some of the Nazi guards were disappearing. They were taking off their uniforms, putting on ordinary clothes and running away.

Realising that Germany was losing the war, the guards were frightened of being taken captive themselves! The two RAF pilots realised this could be a chance for them to escape. They forced their way out one night and stole one of the cars from the camp. They decided only to drive at night as they did not know whether Holland had been liberated yet. They stole petrol from farm tractors and hid in the woods and farm sheds during the daylight hours. They were lucky never to be found by anyone.

The only food they had would be what they could find growing in the fields, like turnips or the sort of food fed to cattle. Sometimes if they were really lucky, they might find some nuts or even the odd apple on the trees.

It was early that morning as they entered Belgium they realised it had been liberated, not a German in sight. They were delirious with happiness when they saw me and realised I could speak English! I took them into the Mess where they received a great welcome and they ate an enormous breakfast. When they had finished, the commanding officer asked them what they wanted to do.

'We want to go back to Rotterdam and find the nurses who saved us when we crashed. They pulled us out of our burning aircraft.'

This was obviously something very important to them, so it was decided this must be done. It was at that moment that we heard on the radio the news that peace in Europe had been declared. It was VE Day, Victory in Europe! The whole Mess hall broke into cheers; we all hugged and kissed each other. We were laughing and crying.

We realised too that it was quite safe to travel back to Rotterdam. I was told that I was to go with the two pilots on their travels, together with another WAAF Officer. We packed up an enormous box of food, as we knew how everyone in Holland had been so short of supplies during the German occupation, and we set off in that little Nazi car, still with 'PWX!' painted on it.

It was an exciting journey. The news was being celebrated in all the towns and villages as we passed through. People were in the streets laughing and singing, many with bottles of wine in their hands, offering a glass to those around.

As we arrived at the bank of the river with Rotterdam on the other side, we could see that the bridge connecting it to the city was no longer there. We had a problem. The Germans had destroyed it as they retreated. As we stood there deciding what to do, we noticed a Dutchman in a small boat approaching. As it drew into the landing stage nearby, we asked the man if he would ferry us over to the city. He spoke English quite well, luckily for us, but he shook his head and said it was impossible; the river was mined and with us in it the boat could have hit a mine and that would be it!

He explained he had a flat bottomed boat which was safe enough with just him in it with the supplies of food he would bring over once a week for the starving villages. Even then it was always risky. But he offered to take our box of food and deliver it to the hospital. There was no alternative; we had to agree.

I often think about this and wonder if the food ever got to the nurses. You see there was a black market in food, it was so valuable and that big box full of goodies would be worth a lot of money to the ferryman. I hope they received the food we sent them.

By the time we returned to Malines early that evening, everyone was celebrating – peace in Europe at last after six terrible years. The streets were filled with people, laughing and talking together. I was very tired after being awake for over thirty-six hours and the medical officer looked at me and said I must get some rest. I went back to my billet and climbed into bed but I couldn't sleep. I said to myself: 'This is crazy, the war is over. I want to celebrate!' So I got up, put on a clean uniform and returned to the Mess.

It was buzzing with excitement. Everyone was wondering when they would be returning home. The bar was full of officers celebrating. The medical officer said, 'I thought you would be back.'

We all realised there would be a lot of celebration going on in Brussels, only fifteen kilometres away, so the two pilots and I with another WAAF Officer got back in the little German car and set off for the Belgian capital.

We arrived to a scene of great activity – the streets were full of people celebrating the news, dressed in their best and waving Belgian, British and American Flags. They were singing and dancing and all seemed to have a bottle in their hands. We joined the procession winding its way through the streets heading for the central square. There were Americans in their jeeps, British soldiers, Canadians and some other RAF crews too, so we joined in the fun.

All the residents were lining the roadside waving and shouting with joy. They threw flowers into our vehicles as we passed by and gave us bottles of wine and cakes. The relief of a nation which had been occupied by a cruel enemy and had suffered terribly was only equalled by the joy of the members of the Allied forces who had thoughts of returning home to their loved ones.

It would not be until the early hours of the morning that we returned back to base. I was very sleepy at the beginning, but by the time we returned I was full of beans! Our car was filled with flowers, bottles, cakes and ribbons they had thrown to us and the two pilots who were overwhelmed with happiness at being free. It had been a long day for us all.

That was a night I will never forget.

CHAPTER TWENTY-THREE

We thought we would all be sent home very soon after the end of war in Europe but it was not to be. We were told we had to help Belgium get back on its feet and would be given other duties. I never could have imagined what was in store for me.

Because I spoke French reasonably well, I was told I was to go to Breendonk every day for three weeks and show different groups of RAF personnel around, acting as a guide and translator. Fort Breendonk was a concentration camp known as the Camp of Silence and of Death. I was totally surprised and a little anxious. I wondered what had happened there and what I was going to see.

Breendonk was a small village outside Brussels in Belgium. A fort had been built there just before the First

World War as part of the defence of Antwerp. When the Germans occupied Belgium during the war, they took over the fort and converted it into a concentration camp.

On September 20th, 1940, a particularly cruel and vicious SS officer, Lager Commandant Philip Schmitt brought his first victims to Breendonk. It became a transit camp for Jews, a place to keep the people before they were sent elsewhere. They eventually made up over half the number of prisoners there and would then be sent on to the extermination camps, such as Auschwitz. Soon afterwards, it became the place where political prisoners like Communists and members of the Belgian Resistance were held. They also imprisoned gay people and anyone who they considered to have deformities.

When Chief Commandant Schmitt took over control at Breendonk, it became one of the most infamous and feared camps of all, despite being quite small. He was known to keep a fierce and nasty a dog which would attack the prisoners. But this was the least of their tortures.

The camp had been closed in August 1944, as the Allies made their way through France, and the remaining prisoners were sent to Auschwitz.

I didn't know any of this history when I arrived. Neither did I realise that the prisoners exercising in the courtyard as I walked through were the Flemish traitors who had joined the Germans. They were mostly in their late teens and their twenties and stared at me as I passed. They were reputed to be even crueller to their own people than the Nazis. After their post-war trial, most of these men were either executed or imprisoned for life.

As I arrived, I saw a high wall of earth around the building. It was impossible to see at first what was behind it. Then I entered the main gates and went over the road bridging a moat. The main gates were huge and I had to ring a large bell outside. As it clanged, I felt a shiver go down my spine. What would I find inside?

The door was eventually opened by a man in uniform. I showed him my pass and explained what I was ordered to do. He nodded sternly and took me to meet the officer in charge, who spoke in French and was relieved when I could understand him. He said the Fort was not open normally to outsiders as it was now holding many of the Belgian traitors as prisoners. However, he had been asked to allow the RAF to be given access for the next few weeks.

I explained that I was to show groups of RAF personnel what had happened within these walls. The local RAF commander in Belgium had decided that as many as possible should be shown this camp and learn of the terrible events that had taken place. My grim task was to escort these groups each day and tell them what had taken place there.

I asked my guide to tell me the history of the wartime years there. I was shocked at his story.

About 3,500 prisoners had passed through this camp including thirty women and they all suffered what a Belgian writer describes as 'The Hell of Breendonk.' Few survived. They were starved, executed, or sent to the concentration camps to certain death.

My guide added, 'I was lucky – I was one of the few survivors.' He had worked for the Belgian Resistance, the underground movement who sent information to our intelligence agents, risking his life every moment, a brave man.

My vivid memories of the camp will never leave me.

The prisoners lived in concrete bunkers that had no heating. Their sleeping quarters were designed for thirty, but housed double that number. The bunks were three tiered and they slept on straw mattresses. In the daytime, their toilets were two trenches in the main courtyard; they were only allowed to stay for two minutes. Many of the non-Jewish prisoners had been in the Resistance. They would be put in solitary confinement cells to make them give up information, with open-grilled ceilings like bird cages. They had two meals a day served through a hole in the door. In order to eat, their hands would be freed but they had to lie on the floor to reach the food, like animals.

On the walls of the punishment cells the prisoners had written messages in blood. One had left a message saying he had been betrayed by his mistress and he wrote her name, Leonardine Boissons; another prisoner had made marks on the wall for every day he was imprisoned there – six straight vertical lines and one diagonal – one more week of captivity. One prisoner must have been an artist; he had drawn a face of Christ on the chalk wall. My memories of these cells are still vivid to this day.

The RAF personnel, all men, who I escorted round every day wondered why they had been sent there, but by the end of the two hour visit they realised that they should know the reason for fighting this war and what terrible acts had been committed there by the enemy.

I had to go there every day for three weeks – three weeks that I will never forget – where I saw man's cruelty to man.

CHAPTER TWENTY-FOUR

Finally my stay in Belgium came to end. It was late June 1945, and I had not seen my husband for six months, except for one brief hour when I was flown to RAF Northolt air base where he was stationed. We both wrote letters saying how sad we were to be apart but we had to bear it.

In July, I returned back to Fighter Command Headquarters at Stanmore. I would now at least be able to see more of Peter whenever he got time off, as RAF Northolt was not too far away. I wondered how we would get on after all those months apart. I had only known him for nine months, and had left only three months after we had married. I also wondered what new job I would be given as we were told we would not be demobbed from the WAAF (that means to become a civilian again) for some time yet.

Returning to my normal admin duties at 33 Wing gave me a strange feeling – I felt as though all the horrors at Breendonk were just a dream.

I was in for another surprise. I was told I was going on a course called 'Learning How to Teach'. I would have to leave my husband again after only two weeks.

I had no idea what I was to teach, or who would be my students. I spent the next three weeks in a camp in the West Country with ten other people. The training was very intense. We learned how to gain the attention of our students, we were taught to explain things carefully. I found it fascinating, but still I did not know who or what I would be teaching.

Our final test came. We had to give a demonstration lesson and show what we had learned. We were given a pound note to buy supplies for our lesson, and told that the talk would last for half an hour. We could choose our own subject for the test. I decided to talk about herbs in cookery so I took my pound and went to a shop and bought three tea towels, all with pictures of herbs on them.

I gave my talk and was passed as a suitable teacher and sent back to Stanmore. I would be teaching a group of famous and very brave Polish pilots, including one who had been a pilot in the First World War. They had managed to escape when their country was occupied, in order to continue the fight. The Polish pilots had the highest records of kills during the war. They knew what the German invasion would mean for Poland.

They came to Britain knowing they might never be able to return to their homeland, and possibly would never see their families again. Now they wanted to stay in Britain and make a new life for themselves, hoping their families would join them. During their time here, they picked up some sort of English but they had terrible accents and used all sorts of words and phrases that were only words we used in the Air Force. Words like 'wizard prang' when you shot an enemy down, 'angels' to describe how high you were flying, and 'pongo' for an

Army officer, wouldn't be very helpful when these Polish officers were trying to make their way in Britain after the war.

I wondered how I could help them and then I remembered I had learned something called shorthand. This was a way of writing down anything someone was dictating to you in special signs that were quicker than ordinary writing. Every sign represented a sound in our language.

I used shorthand to teach them all the different sounds we used speaking English, all the short and long vowels like 'a' and 'ah', and the different syllables – how to pronounce 'kn' in knock and 'ing' at the end of a word. Gradually they improved and we had a lot of fun on the way, as they began to speak something we could understand.

I gave them lessons every afternoon for five months and then it was time for me to be demobbed and released from the Air Force. Peter's father had given us a flat over the stables, so I could stay there to wait until Peter was also released.

From then onwards, the Polish officers would come to my flat and have their lessons there. I was paid twenty-eight shillings, that is £1.40 today, for every lesson and it still kept me in touch with the RAF. Then they too were demobbed and had to leave and make their way as new British citizens. I wonder what happened to them. On their last day, they presented me with a lovely book, signed by them all. It was entitled *Poland's Progress.* I still remember those brave men and wonder whether they were ever able to see their families again.

Peter finally received the date when he would leave the Air Force, just two days before our son was born in March. At last we were ready to start life in a peaceful world as a family. But how could we earn a living? We had to eat, and buy clothes and lots of other things for the fast-approaching baby. Peter had worked in making films before the war, but there were fewer films being made now and no chance of getting back into that industry. Although I had worked in the centre of London pre-war, no women were employed if they were married and had children. I had to think what to do to increase our income.

Peter, still stationed at Northolt, was only home on the occasional night, and my new in-laws were practically strangers to me. The Stanmore Riding School was always busy. My father-in-law was in great demand for providing horses and carriages for all the film studios around – Pinewood and Elstree amongst them – and taught a number of famous actors and actresses how to ride for films too.

Every Sunday he famously organised a morning ride. Many well-known business men would meet and take part in a two-hour ride across the Stanmore Common and around the farms, ending at the Vine pub, which had been used during the war as the favourite haunt of the Fighter Command pilots.

I realised it was up to me to do something to give my life a meaning. Peter's family were good with horses, but not so good at keeping accounts. His mother, Tommy, did all the office work and accounts as well as looking after the students and organising the daily rides, so I offered to take on that job which gave me plenty to do.

Meanwhile, Peter had managed to find a sales representative post with Quaker Oats, going around the farms and selling their special animal feed products. They provided a car so at least we had transport. But he also kept his fellow musicians from the Air Force together and formed a dance orchestra called 'Peter Younghusband and his Music'.

In March 1946, our son was born. We named him Clive Francis Younghusband. As he grew up, Clive would sit in his pram in the stable yard and watch the horses as they came and went. He even learned to ride when he was four years old. I loved him dearly but after six years of coping with the challenges of war and having such big responsibilities since the age of nineteen, I couldn't just stay at home. I wondered if I would ever find anything to fill this need.

When Clive was a little older, we spent a holiday with a cousin of Peter's mother who owned a small hotel in a remote corner of north Devon. It was surrounded with farmland that provided most of the customers. It was a truly beautiful spot, and we thoroughly enjoyed our first holiday together.

Back home at Stanmore a month later, we were surprised to receive a letter from the owners. They were planning to buy another hotel in Wincanton, and asked if we would like to come and run the hotel in Devon. Of course we knew nothing about hotel-keeping, but neither of us was really enjoying our current work so, after a very short discussion, we said yes.

You never knew who would come in the door; it could be a pop star or an actor. One day, a future prime minister came through the door. It was Edward Heath, who was also a Territorial Officer. His regiment were at camp nearby and used us for several years for their annual regimental camp dinner. We met new people from different countries and backgrounds every day.

Peter and I spent our days working hard, but finding it interesting as well. We rose to our new challenge. Our war years gave us the strength and ability to search for any opportunity that life might present, and the confidence to grasp it with both hands.

A LITTLE BIT MORE

Now that I am ninety-five years old, I look back on the years I spent as a member of WAAF and I have mixed feelings. I remember all the aircrews we lost in the bombing raids and the fighter aircraft that were shot down.

I am proud of the way young women filled the roles of men who joined up, and did incredible work. I especially think of the girls who worked with me in the Filter Room who had boyfriends, brothers and husbands in the aircrews that we tracked as they went out to fight. The girls knew which squadrons were operating and knew those their loved ones served in. But they also knew how many planes didn't make it back after an operation.

There were bad days when someone received news of the loss of someone dear to them and good days when they heard that they were alive. Despite everything, they always turned up for duty on time and did their job like professionals. They were superb.

Even now, some days remain in my memory. I will never forget the sights of ruined homes in London after a night of heavy bombing, the sound of the explosions as the bombs landed, and the devastating effects of the V2s that landed on Antwerp.

I remember learning to shoot Sten guns with my friends and laughing at the complaints of the fishermen who were accidently peppered by our shots. I think of my friends who died and of George, the man I might have married.

I seem to have crammed a lifetime of experiences into those war years. I used to wonder what the coming years would bring after the excitement of life in the Filter Rooms, although of course I hoped there would never be another world war, that the world had learned its lesson. It saddens me to know that soldiers are still fighting, lives are still being lost, and many are suffering the loss of their loved ones to battle.

After the war, I kept the promise that I made when I signed the Official Secrets Act in 1940 and didn't tell a soul of the work done in the Filter Rooms. My husband Peter never found out about my role, and was never able to be proud as I am of those in the RDF chain.

Now, I am delighted that the world knows our story. RAF Fighter Command Headquarters at Bentley Priory, where I spent the last of my war years, has become a museum which commemorates Air Chief Marshal Sir Hugh Dowding, the aircrew members, and the Radar Ops, and Filter personnel 'the one, the few, the many'.

Bentley Priory Museum was opened in 2013 by Prince Charles and I was given the job of telling him how it worked. The efforts of those involved in the Radar chain are now truly being recognised. I was even recently given the privilege of taking part in a BBC documentary series titled *Britain's Greatest Generation*.

It seems you're not too old in your nineties to begin a television career.

Among all the tragedy and loss, those terrible years gave us the sense of loyalty we all felt to our country, and the determination that we would win the war. These qualities have helped us in the difficult times post war; discipline, punctuality and pulling together as a team.

The years march on; every day new experiences, new challenges. I have tried to make up for the things I missed out on in the war years; I have travelled to many countries, learned new languages and finally achieved a university degree (even if I did have to wait until I was eighty-eight years old!).

I have written books and enjoy giving talks to schools and other organisations to share my story. I have campaigned for adult education, and even found time to feature in a documentary or two. I wake up each day wondering what excitement it will bring.

I was nineteen when I joined the Women's Auxilliary Air Force, eighty-eight when I completed my degree, and ninety-two when I received a British Empire Medal for services to lifelong education. Who knows what will be next. I've learned that you're never too old – or too young – to make a difference.

Winning the People's Book Prize
for *One Woman's War* (read it when you're older!)

A CHAT WITH EILEEN

HOW DO YOU PREPARE TO WRITE A BOOK?

When I start writing, I'm always at my big table in the office. I never write in the living room. When I begin my writing, first of all I write by hand. I start by jotting headlines of what I want to cover, and only then when I've got the bones of it I go out to the computer, which is in front of a big window looking out on to the garden and the Penarth countryside. Then I can transfer my notes and headlines onto the computer, and I go from there.

WHO DID YOU MEET DURING THE WAR THAT INSPIRED YOU?

There have been lots of people in my life who have done this, my father for example. He was in the First World War, and he had always had a tough life, but he taught me to never give up, and that inspired me to keep moving forward.

Naturally, I was influenced by the Royal Air Force officers – Wing Commander Rudd was a special one. He was the officer who picked me out after just three months, and offered me the chance to be promoted to an officer.

IF YOU COULD GO BACK AND RE-LIVE ONE DAY FROM YOUR LIFE. WHICH DAY WOULD YOU PICK?

I don't think there is one day in particular. I would say I'd like to go back to any day when I was apprehensive or waiting for news. This time if I could go back, knowing that it would be good news, I wouldn't do anything differently but I wouldn't suffer so much!

THERE HAVE BEEN HUNDREDS OF CHANGES IN TECHNOLOGY OVER THE YEARS. WHAT NEW INVENTION DO YOU THINK HAS BEEN THE MOST IMPORTANT?

I think that computers and the Internet have been really important, but also there has been a huge development in different types of aircraft. When I flew during the war planes were much slower, the speed just wasn't there. A lot of the development in aircraft has come from war-time, the technology that was first developed as Radar helped a lot in further development of air travel.

WHAT ARE YOUR FAVOURITE HOBBIES, OTHER THAN WRITING?

My hobby used to be playing hockey. I played for the county, and I played for the Royal Air Force during the war. Now, I suppose its meeting people. I quite enjoy being invited to give talks about my experiences, because every time it's a new challenge. You never know what the audience are going to be like. Sometimes people are very quiet and just like listening, others ask lots of questions.

IF YOU COULD GIVE ADVICE TO CHILDREN ABOUT WAR, WHAT WOULD IT BE?

I think one thing is very important to know: Don't give in to fear. Better to think what you can do to help; learn new languages and new skills. We learned how to make food rations stretch, and how to grow what food we could. When there is a war, you must face it head on.

HAVING LIVED THROUGH WORLD WAR TWO, HOW DO YOU THINK IT CHANGED YOU?

The war certainly changed my life. It took me out of a quiet life in a London suburb, and allowed me to travel to lots of different countries. I met all sorts of people I wouldn't have met otherwise; it presented challenges that I wouldn't have faced. Probably more than anything else, the war showed me how life can change overnight. Mine certainly did. I probably wouldn't have known my potential, living a quiet life in north London.

DID YOU MAKE ANY FRIENDS WHO YOU STAYED IN TOUCH WITH DURING THE WAR?

People came from many different backgrounds and most went their separate ways after the war. I'm still in touch with a friend of mine called Pat Robins. She's actually the daughter of a famous writer Denise Robins, and Pat writes, too. I remember watching her on the night watch, where sometimes nothing would happen for two or three hours. She would sit there with pencil and paper writing stories. She used to send them up to magazines and got money for them, I think twelve pounds a story. She saved up and bought a little white car, and we used to go up to London in it. I was with Pat in her car when we met Dylan Thomas – he was always very cheeky! Pat and I are still in touch today.

IF YOU COULD CHANGE ANYTHING ABOUT THE WORLD TODAY WHAT WOULD IT BE?

I think we should all make more effort to learn other languages, just to try and understand people a bit. We shouldn't just expect everybody to speak English! Also, I think that we shouldn't be so focused on money and possessions. People can often become quite greedy, but I think the world would be better if people valued other things more.

WERE YOU EVER REALLY AFRAID?

I think I felt nervous more than afraid. I felt apprehensive when I got my first job and had to travel up to London on the train every day by myself, it was quite scary for a young girl! When I was working in Belgium, outside the office in Mechelen there was actually a V2 that hadn't gone off. Why we were allowed to have the bomb there I don't know! We always said to one another, 'I wonder if it will go off?' We used to pat it as we walked out the door – 'Hi, matey, keep quiet!'

DID YOU HAVE A FAVOURITE FILM OR TELEVISION PROGRAMME?

There wasn't any television during the war, but sometimes we would go to the cinema. I didn't like love stories, I liked travel films. I always wanted to travel. I thought that when I set off for France I would carry on .

WHAT IS YOUR FAVOURITE SONG OF ALL TIME?

Toreador from Carmen. I've always enjoyed opera music

– I remember learning to play Toreador on the piano when I was younger.

WHAT IS THE PROUDEST MOMENT IN YOUR LIFE?

Probably when I met Prince Charles and Camilla and made him laugh! They were due to open the Bentley Priory Museum at Fighter Command Headquarters. I'd sent a copy of my previous book *One Woman's War* to him in the weeks before, and I had written to say I was going to meet him, and I thought it would be a good idea if he knew a bit about the background of the Filter Rooms. On the day, Prince Charles asked me, 'What exactly were you doing here?' I looked right at him and said, 'You didn't read my book, did you?' Prince Charles roared with laughter, looked to Camilla and said, 'Darling, Eileen is telling me off for not reading her book!' There is a photograph somewhere of me wagging my finger at him. It was very funny, and I was extremely proud to have raised a laugh.

Also available from Candy Jar Books

AMULET

by Alison Thomas

A magical story of cave dwellers, clowns and vegetarian dragons.

Dion has Asperger's Syndrome. He is an intelligent boy who lives in the functional ordered world.

When he is kidnapped and taken to a place beyond the imagination, Dion finds that his disciplined mind becomes strength. But little does he realise his life is now in danger.

Will his sister Megan get to him in time? Not if the evil Queen has anything to do with it.

For a boy who doesn't like change. Dion's strength and determination is the one thing he will have to rely on.

ISBN: 978-0-9933221-6-7

Also available from Candy Jar Books

THINNER THAN WATER

by Sue Hampton

Kim Braddock and Fizzy Duvall have never met. Kim's a passionate footballer with a repertoire of impressions, a temper and a dark sense of humour. Fizzy's a shy, romantic idealist who wants to please everyone.

All they have in common is a very big city, one black parent and one white – and the same fifteenth birthday.

When their identities are overturned, they form a bond that changes them both as two families struggle with the truth. But as conflict deepens, is their connection strong enough to survive?

Fiction for young adults aged 13+

"Thinner Than Water is an enjoyable and fascinating read. This is a fantastic template for an onscreen drama."
Beverley Knight

ISBN: 978-0-9931191-0-1

Also available from Candy Jar Books

Tommy Parker: Destiny Will Find You

by Anthony Ormond

When Tommy Parker packs his bag and goes to his grandpa's house for the summer he has no idea that his life is about to change forever.

But that's exactly what happens when his grandpa lets him in on a fantastic secret. He has a pen that lets him travel through his own memories and alter the past. Imagine that! Being able to travel into your own past and re-write your future.

Tommy Parker: Destiny Will Find You! is an exhilarating adventure that redefines the time travel genre.

You'll never look at your memories in quite the same way again…

ISBN: 978-0-9928607-1-4

Also available from Candy Jar Books

DOCTOR WHO EDITION

Space, Time, Machine, Monster: Doctor Who Edition takes you on a journey into the science of *Doctor Who.*

Jam-packed with aliens, time machines, spaceships and lots of monsters, this book explores the secrets of the Universe's favourite Time Lord.

And, for an extra bit of fun, we present our own *Doctor Who* Top 10s on topics such as planets, companions, favourite stories and catchphrases!

So how does a Dalek poo? Let's find out!

ISBN: 978-0-9933221-3-6